living modern

living modern:
the sourcebook
of contemporary
interiors

richard powers
text by phyllis richardson

with 740 color illustrations

Thames & Hudson

introduction

Long live the good taste manifested by choice, subtlety, proportion and harmony.

LE CORBUSIER

What does it mean to be modern? It is not strictly a style, but rather an attitude to style, one that is less purist and more creative than you might imagine. To create a modern space is to take in the full panoply of international references, to consider place and climate, form and function, and to invent inspired environments that adapt easily to modern living.

The word 'modern' is no longer weighted with expectations that predict, with regard to interiors, a regime of stark white and chrome, or purely functional spaces that are conceived as 'machines for living'. Modernism, as it was practised in architecture and design in the 20th century, was about newness, using the best new methods and materials to their full advantage, rather than adhering to past traditions and styles. Being modern was always about having a wide rather than a narrow view. Taking this original definition of the word allows us to consider a much broader spectrum of styles, influences, principles and techniques that still sits happily within the sophisticated design zeitgeist of the 21st century.

While such an approach could result in the amalgamation of just about any category of furnishings and objects, the modern style is grounded firmly in harmony of proportion, in the balance between architecture and decoration, between pattern and texture, between colour and light. The aesthetic established by Mies van der Rohe in, for example, his Barcelona Pavilion (1929) set the pace, though not the prescription, for modern style: here, interlocking panes of white travertine, green Tinian marble and pure glass show that simple does not have to mean plain or in any way boring, and that

a backdrop composed of extraordinary materials can make the most elegant setting for much-loved objects, furniture and works of art. While Mies' use of unembellished stone and glass was a challenge to the more effusive decorating sensibilities that preceded him, its greater significance is in promoting the idea that a beautiful surface can be its own decoration.

In these pages you will see similarly blank planes made of exotic wood, textured concrete, weathered steel. But instead of Mies' specially designed pieces, the furniture might be a velvet-covered sofa, the object a coloured, injection-moulded bookcase, the work of art an African tribal sculpture. You wouldn't see these things in the Barcelona Pavilion but you will see them in a contemporary modern interior. And while the backdrops might be intricate and beautiful, they also leave room for inspired variation and expression.

Another aspect of the modern interior is the fluid arrangement of spaces, which liberates us from the confinement of walled rooms for each function. Living areas are defined not only by walls, but also by partitions that articulate rooms without enclosing them; or a wall might be composed not only of a large sheet of glass but also of the lush planting beyond, which becomes an essential part of the interior environment and colour scheme.

Today's interior might also have robust patterns on the walls, for example, decorative wallpaper, something that many devotees of Modernism would not countenance. But the modern sensibility can use pattern to make beautifully nuanced interiors that are nothing like the many layers of printed curtains and fabrics and decorative wall-coverings of old. The successful modern interior features a considered juxtaposition of elements, of what is next to the wall-covering, what complements rather than distracts. A space might have vines criss-crossing the walls, but this pattern will take precedence while other elements are downplayed: there are no riots of competing patterns or colours, but a few objects that interact with the wall decoration and perhaps tease out pleasing resonances that might otherwise be lost among an array of textiles and objects.

There is, admittedly, an element of minimalism that carries through these interiors, in that any very decorative piece is usually allowed a solo performance while other characters in the room are kept to more muted notes. It is a question of harmony, or balance, between stronger and more subdued elements, which creates an interior that is pleasantly calming rather than overwhelming.

Because of the numerous aspects that make up these spaces, because enjoying the sense of balance

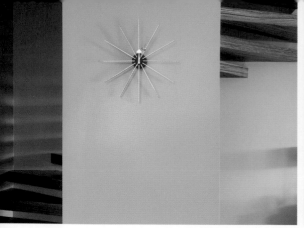

means having components to balance and not just paring anything decorative away until only structure is left, this book is arranged into sections that explore the many different elements with which modern interiors are created. In search of the most ingeniously stylish and richly modern spaces anywhere, this is a book of some of the most stunning interiors from around the world.

The first section of the book, Place, considers the wide variety of contexts and relationships to setting in which the modern home can happily exist. Alongside the minimal New York loft apartments are bold contemporary houses in the Australian outback; timber houses in lush tropical landscapes in Singapore, Sri Lanka and Bali; jungle retreats and tower-block apartments in Brazil; hillside perches in Los Angeles and San Francisco; desert bungalows and urban penthouses, French chateaux and Italian villas. By showing some of these houses or apartments in their settings we hope to dispel the idea that place determines character, but at the same time to demonstrate how the use of materials and architecture can take best advantage of, or integrate with, environment, natural light and climate.

Style focuses on interiors that follow a particular theme, such as mid-century modern, sleek minimal or high rustic. But here, too, the definitions are loose and the examples demonstrate that themes can be used to help bring unity and need not be seen as strict limitations. This holds true also for the nature of the structure. Within the section entitled Architecture we are not looking at the overall style of building – we do show some beautiful examples of contemporary architecture by known practitioners – but at discrete aspects of the architecture that inform the arrangement and flow of the interiors. These include such design specifics as open-plan living spaces, double-height volumes and indoor–outdoor design, along with features such as hallways and balconies that are part of the structure of the building.

Of course, there is a lot of opportunity for overlap and most of the images will contain a mixture of elements that help to create the whole. That mix is, of course, the point. In the Materials section, windows and stairs, for example, are part of the architecture of the house, and they will also reveal the materials of which the rooms are composed. But the intrinsic characters of materials deserve their own separate focus, since the range of houses and apartments, farms and cottages across the globe will be constructed from many combinations and forms of wood, glass, steel, brick, stone, plaster or other materials. Glass can be pure planes or bricks; wood polished, rough or planked; steel weathered or burnished. The materials and

treatments selected for cladding on walls and ceilings, as flooring or partitions will have a tremendous influence on the interior spaces, as well as on the house's external character.

From materials we proceed logically to surfaces, which is something we considered separately from materials in terms of texture and feel. Because in some cases, no matter what the material, it is the way it is rendered, whether rough or smooth, soft or hard, that helps determine the style and ambience of a room.

Function presents rooms according to their conventional use, but also asks how such spaces might be considered in more contemporary or unexpected ways, giving new interpretations of bedrooms, living rooms or kitchens to demonstrate how function may be strictly interpreted or loosely flaunted.

Ambience deals with perhaps the most subtle aspects of an interior scheme. These include more abstract qualities, such as natural light, the use of white, neutral or colourful tones, the effects of screens and patterns, as in wallpaper, and rooms centred around the alluring warmth of an open fire.

The next section, Elements, considers the large and small influences of internal architectural details in a room, such as stairs or storage units, and the shape and size of window openings, as well as

smaller details such as lighting, fixtures and objets d'art. These are the specific, definable components that are both functional and convey a good overall sense of style.

The section on Furniture provides an opportunity to look closely at individual choices of furnishings and furniture arrangements, including a remarkable array of modern and iconic masterpieces as well as retro designs, vintage, antique and ethnic pieces, all assembled with a modern eye for editing and composition.

Lastly, we look at the Outdoors, not from a gardener's perspective – though in some cases the gardens are themselves modern works of art – but to explore the concept of seamless living that overflows from within walls onto terraces, through open courtyards and around outdoor cooking and eating spaces.

Looking at each of these concepts separately gives us a better understanding of how they work together to produce beautiful spaces that are well suited to modern living, an approach that is less confined in organization, function and space than the habits of preceding generations. It calls for interiors that are creative and inspiring, drawn from a rich store of influences and adapted to our sophisticated, flexible and global lifestyles.

place

The modern approach to design transcends geographic boundaries and uses the best methods from across the globe. But we are often intrigued to know how a house or apartment sits in context, to visualize the palm trees swaying, the view across the hillside or the city lights winking all around. We get a sense of what home means in different places and perhaps wake up to our own landscape. The modern style is adaptable to almost any context, so the uncluttered interiors that make the best use of space, light and proportion are advantageous in all climates, but they also carry specific benefits for each.

city
16

desert
18

forest
22

water
26

mountain & hillside
30

remote
34

tropical
38

When we come across a beautiful interior in a house or an apartment, sometimes the first thing we want to know is: Where is it? Is it in a town, in the country, on a beach? A property's worth, we are often told, is tied up with location. But in a selection of some of the most remarkable houses in locations all over the world, place seems not to be a restrictive condition. Sometimes we want to know where a house is just so that we can determine whether that particular interior arrangement can work for our own spaces. This is not a limiting exercise, however; looking at the range of design styles in different settings expands the view of what is possible and the repertoire of potential styles and solutions for any location.

In order to present a wide assortment of great interiors with multifarious interpretations of what it means to be modern, we have included houses, apartments, villas, chateaux, rural retreats and urban pieds-à-terre. We look at how a house sits in the thick greenery of a forest, the tangled vegetation of a tropical jungle, the arid landscape of the desert. There are distinctly Modernist boxes in open remote settings and cabins that adhere to the wood-clad vernacular, though are modern in shape and function.

Urban or rural contexts are often the easiest to discern in a living space, since wide-open countryside tends to inspire greater room inside, and the crowded confines of the city require solutions that make a virtue of minimal floor area. But, as we know, these assumptions do not always hold true. An open-plan loft apartment can be made to feel more expansive than a rural farmhouse surrounded by acres of land. Although a cosy mountain cottage will probably contain small, intimate spaces, wonderfully warm spots from which to contemplate the great outdoors just beyond, it may also make use of advanced thermal glazing products so that giant windows frame the wilderness outside. These unexpected twists, grand gestures or discrete variations, though they may deviate from the notion of what is fitting in a certain area, are usually the elements that emphasize an extraordinary location while making its unique demands seem less like a limitation and more of an opportunity for experimentation and surprise.

Most of the examples here combine a conscious bow to situation and climate with the modern awareness of space. They also present some innovative designs that help to maintain the modern flow of space and light even in their very particular conditions. A Modernist-style glass-walled house on Sydney Harbour makes indoor and outdoor an almost seamless transition by using modern building methods to create a stable foundation next to a large body of water. A desert house makes the landscape part of its structure with a boulder that protrudes into the living space. Other hillside houses may be hidden in surrounding greenery or extend seemingly into free air, but all make the most of spectacular views. In desert areas, where the indoor–outdoor scheme is aided by weather but often disadvantaged by lack of greenery or by plantings that require a lot of maintenance to thrive, the creative use of native plants helps maximize the potential of a garden so that the outdoor space is still inclusive and welcoming. A hillside house in Santa Barbara, California, not far from the urban conurbation in miles travelled but light years away in feel, takes full advantage of its setting and vistas and includes a swimming pool that holds extra water supplies in case of wildfires. An open-air house in Bali makes native palms and ferns part of the decor, while modern reflecting pools mimic the soothing murmur of the rainforest streams.

Sometimes location will impart a certain character to a dwelling, which can successfully be exploited by the design. Houses built on a hillside or mountain slope carry an immediate sense of drama. From the outside the structure will appear to have a precarious existence, while inside, the knowledge of walking on a cantilevered floor space heightens the excitement of the view into the open air beyond the living room windows, or from a deck that appears to float above the treetops. Similarly, a loft apartment with an open-plan interior and large windows on the city has a distinctly glamorous ambience, as will a strikingly modern house in an otherwise wild tropical setting. And a cottage surrounded by ancient trees, rugged hills or a windswept vista will embody the idea of shelter and comfort. All of these things are true and yet the modern variations will make each situation even more remarkable to experience and inhabit.

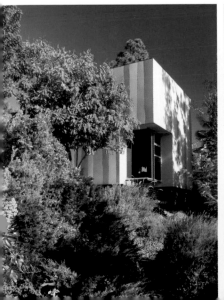

city

City living may mean sacrificing some space and greenery, but modern thinking makes interiors feel more spacious by using creative solutions wherever possible. With our new awareness of the environment, green roofs and living walls are becoming more prevalent in cities, helping to minimize the overheated effects of concrete, brick and asphalt. The most successful rooms in urban dwellings tend to be those that either embrace the views and the ambience of the city or those that offer a secluded respite from it.

Nothing provides an antidote to urban grit like a peaceful private terrace (below). This indoor–outdoor living space could easily be part of a sprawling suburban retreat but the fact of its being in an urban centre makes it a joy to experience. Fashion designer Donna Karan's New York apartment (opposite) makes the most of a view across Central Park to that world-famous skyline. The solid wood benches and plants make the space feel more like a relaxed picnic area than a confined high-rise terrace.

desert

There was a time when people moved to the desert for the space and fresh air but tried to bring the trappings of cooler climes along with them. Thirsty vegetation from regions of abundant snow and rainfall struggled in desert soil, and clapboard houses were poor protection from fluctuations between high desert sun and cold nights. As it moved westward, American architecture tried to retain its genteel East Coast traditions. Later, the International Style, with its use of massive glass walls and overhanging roofs, embraced and exploited the desert landscape. This classic Modernist house built by Albert Frey in Palm Springs, California, in 1964, takes a giant boulder into its structure, where it assumes a sculptural presence in the living and dining areas. The glass walls on all sides offer clear views across the desert floor to the mountains beyond.

Modern desert architecture tends to favour the low horizontal bungalow style that eschews second-floor rooms, where heat becomes trapped. Controlled window openings in a house in Dubai (left) protect the interior from harsh direct sunlight in a region where temperatures often reach 41° Celsius in summer. The vegetation is very sparse so any structure must provide its own shade. A house built in the desert of southern California (opposite) shows the more recent influence of the International Style. Here the large windows and sheltered patio allow the house to be open to the breeze, while the low profile and overhanging roof help minimize heat gain. Native scrub and yucca plants surround the large swimming pool, which appears like an oasis in the dry landscape.

forest

The forest setting immediately calls to mind words like 'enchanted', 'peaceful' and 'secluded'. Whether you are in a tropical rainforest or alpine thicket, being surrounded by trees is somehow comforting and liberating, protective and inspiring in equal measure. For a modern house the forest becomes part of the interior through large windows and accessible outdoor spaces.

A rural retreat sits hidden in the forest of Pennsylvania (opposite, left), surrounded by acres of uninhabited land. Fashion designer Jenny Kee's holiday home (opposite, right) in the Blue Mountains of Australia, an area of deep woodland, sandy plateaus and soaring rock towers, is perched on the hillside and features an open porch overlooking wild native vegetation.

A new-build house in coastal parkland north of Brisbane (below, left) steps up a steep hillside to take in the view, while another house in the Australian bush (below, right) sits within the trees. The camouflaged façade belies the soaring interior spaces.

More forest homes and retreats hidden in the trees. An island weekend home near Sydney is sheltered by giant eucalyptus (below). The island was formerly an artists' colony and there are no private cars. Fashion and interiors designer Todd Oldham built a cottage retreat in the woods of northeast Pennsylvania and then added this object of childhood fantasy (opposite). The treehouse is supported by several mature trunks and accessed by an open wood stair. The designer kept to rustic materials, using lots of unfinished wood inside and out. A walkway/deck with lodgepole railings surrounds the house and offers an open platform in the trees.

water

Human beings are naturally drawn to and fascinated by water. One of the most famous houses ever built straddles a 9m (30ft) waterfall – Frank Lloyd Wright's Fallingwater in Pennsylvania. Architects and designers continue to experiment with designs that capture wide views of sea, lake and river. Others are interested in the idea of making a house appear to float over or near the surface. This house overlooking Sydney Harbour (below) sits low on the shoreline, giving the feeling of being on the water. A hillside house has a spectacular view over Lake Zurich (opposite, top right), while on the other side of the world, a house in Singapore features elegant dockside access (opposite, top left). A mountain retreat on the northeast coast of America mimics the style of traditional barn buildings and looks onto a rocky pond (opposite, bottom right), while an Australian house also reaches out to a pond (opposite, bottom left).

A glass-and-steel house that utilizes industrial components, including roll-up doors (above), sits in groves of olive trees in the mountains near Santa Barbara, California. The shutter doors expose the interior almost completely to the open air. The house faces onto a man-made reservoir that is part swimming pool and part storage facility for water needed in case of wildfires, which are common in the surrounding hills. A modern assemblage of concrete, glass, wood and steel (opposite) makes a distinctively modern composition in an Australian house situated on a waterway. The stair leads to a deck on the roof of the house, while a pool on the opposite side appears to flow into the natural inlet beyond.

mountain & hillside

Mountains and hillsides provide some
of the most dramatic settings for locating
a house. Views are open and vast, and
the steep terrain usually affords a higher
degree of privacy or seclusion than flat
land. The complications of building on
a steep slope do little to put off those who
are determined to live so literally on the
edge. The Garcia House (right) was
designed by John Lautner, one of the most
innovative architects of the last century.
Lautner built many such spectacular
residences that projected themselves
off mountains and hillsides. Their
dramatic locations made them part of film
history: Lautner houses have appeared in
the James Bond and *Die Hard* series. This
house in the hills of Los Angeles could
be on a remote cliff, but its view over
the lights of the city makes it an iconic
urban gem.

The wine country of northern California is an arid, hilly region offering wide open vistas over sparsely inhabited acreage. This hillside cabin (above, left) uses extra-long wood planks to blend with the surrounding mature trees and to emphasize the extension of the deck beyond the ground level. A circular pool appears to hang from the edge of the deck, while another tub offers an open-air spa treatment. Elsewhere, a house in the hills outside of Los Angeles (above, right) feels like a remote hideaway. The hillside position is emphasized with the unfettered glass wall overlooking the cantilevered pool and deck, and chaparral vegetation. A remote winter scene with a house in the Austrian Alps (opposite) recalls the vernacular three-storey arrangement and barn aesthetic.

remote

Remote hideaway or sculptural presence in the landscape, the house that stands alone is still a fantasy for many suburban and urban dwellers. An exuberant, angular addition to Australia's Kangaroo Valley fans out below a clear skyline (opposite). The overhanging roof offers sun shelter and rain protection. The extensive glass walls keep the natural surroundings in constant view. A rural retreat in the Danish countryside (right) comprises a cluster of tidy modern cottages huddled around a common deck and green space for family and friends to enjoy a holiday together. The clapboard siding is in keeping with the local traditional style of building, while the barrel roofs offer space for clerestory windows that bring in more natural light.

The low horizontal profile of a bold modern building embraces its site on Byron Bay, hundreds of miles to the northeast of New South Wales, Australia (above and right). This house on Australia's southern coast (opposite, top) is another example of how a low-profile structure appears to float above the open countryside. A house set in the midst of hundreds of acres of pasture used for a working sheep farm (opposite, bottom) reads like a solid bunker from one direction but on the other side is open to the vast grazing lands.

tropical

The allure of the tropics is not always composed of a rustic native shack sat on a sandy beach. A trend for stark white, high modern structures set against the lush greenery of a tropical jungle has taken hold in recent years, with sublime results. The white rectilinear forms of this thoroughly modern house in the beach resort area of Guarujá, south of São Paulo (below), are softened and enhanced by the sprays of coconut palms. Another example of Brazilian modern (opposite) uses marble tile on the façade to give a warmer tone to the block structure. Here again the native palms become a striking feature set against the hard geometry of the building.

A modern house in Bali (left) is arranged like a series of pavilions around a central courtyard, with outdoor spaces as much a part of the living area as the more fully furnished conventional 'rooms'. Reflecting pools and an outdoor shower carry the theme of water around and through the house. Natural hardwood and old stone are used alongside concrete and glass. In the same house, the old-growth trees of the garden courtyard (below) provide a sense of continuity to a modern design.

style

Here is ample demonstration that modern design comes in a variety of permutations, from rustic to ethnic and baroque expressions. These interiors share a common taste for a somewhat minimal palette, but sometimes the famous pared-down aesthetic is just the beginning, a background on which to display objects and furnishings in vibrant colours or spirited decorative flourishes. The approaches may differ markedly, focusing on modern, antique or vintage elements, or some combination, but the designs are never over-indulged, and the sense of harmony between parts is always more striking than any single element.

Not all interiors are ruled by strict style principles. These days a style can be modern and still incorporate all manner of eccentricities. Not even interiors that strive to be minimalist strictly follow any former dictates of Minimalism. Guided by contemporary sensibilities, and well-schooled in the achievements and shortcomings of pure Modernist design, the designers and residents of these interiors have explored the possibilities of surface materials, as with classic Modernism, and then used them as a backdrop for personal and wide-ranging choices of style arrangements.

While certain styles are familiar, there are others for which we have created terms that set out to describe some popular approaches to interiors that reflect a particularly modern sensibility. For example, since not all modern houses or apartments are located in modern buildings, we need to find a way to describe what happens when good modern design is applied to a stone-walled farmhouse or a rough-hewn cottage. High rustic refers to these interiors where high-quality modern or bold contemporary furnishings sit against a background of natural wood or stone, where more sophisticated pieces of furniture or lighting contrast with unpainted brick or weathered planks. This could be a revamped Mediterranean farmhouse, or a country cottage where 'honest' materials prevail in the construction but furnishings and objects show a taste for more modern, elegant design.

Whether or not it contains mainly furnishings or designs from the 1950s or earlier, the minimal interior retains an adherence to the 'less is more' approach. There is still the feeling that the room contains as few items (and variations) as possible, but today, minimal can also mean the well-judged use of colour and the occasional flourish that maximizes the effect of this much-loved, pared-down interior. A minimal scheme may not have a lot in it, but it can still have a visual impact.

While some are looking for the minimal style, other people look towards the earlier decades of the 20th century with a wider lens, taking in a more comprehensive view of design styles. For devotees of retro design, it is the funkier, colourful elements, the comforting bulky shapes of vintage furnishings and appliances, from postwar, space-age-inspired designs to artifacts of swinging 1970s psychedelia, that draw them in. But while these schemes may

high rustic

The concept of high rustic comes from the idea that even the most modern of us enjoys the age-old charms and atmosphere of historic or vernacular buildings, and wants to preserve those elements and materials that are resonant of their period origins and character. But at the same time we also like to be able to indulge our taste for modern design, not to mention the comforts of functional fittings. A restored farmhouse in rural surroundings outside Santiago in Chile (below and opposite) retains its weathered wood plank walls, which make a mellow background for modern bathroom fittings and classic design pieces such as the Mies van der Rohe Wassily chairs. The wood-burning stove in a corner of the living room and rough-hewn wood low table highlight the simple but artful mix of old and new.

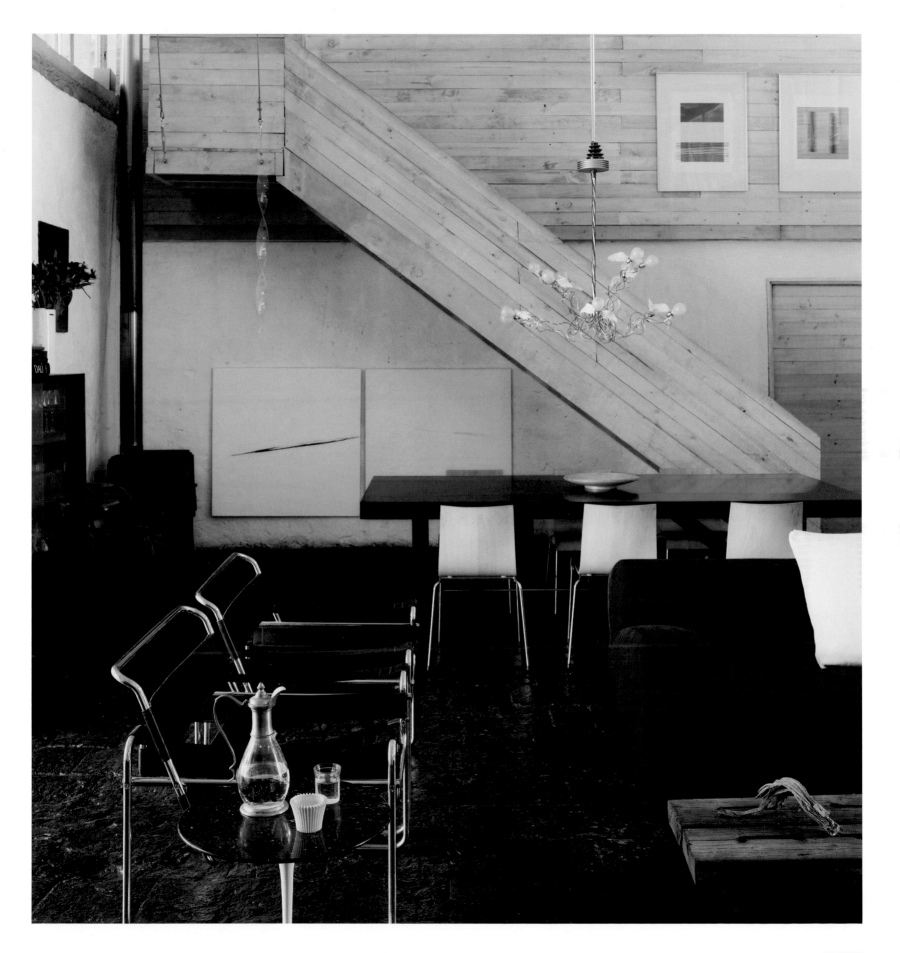

Rustic, not in the rural sense perhaps, but in the centuries-old elements that have been preserved, this London townhouse (above and opposite) combines a taste for spare furnishings and clean open spaces with its heritage. Polished concrete has replaced the old wood-plank floors, and antique dresser and corner cabinets sit alongside Eames dining chairs. The glossy subway tiles and painted wood-panel cupboards contribute to the period ambience. A key modern feature is the abundance of natural light, which makes the contrast between modern and antique that much more perceptible.

minimal

It has earned something of a bad name, an association with interiors that are stark and impersonal, when it was only intended to pare down rooms so that the few items left could be better appreciated. The impact of Minimalism still hovers at the edges of most modern interiors, while in some it has a stronger presence. A Brazilian apartment of large proportions (above, left) showcases mid-century and other modern furniture and objects against a softly draped wall of natural light, while this Paris apartment (above, right) uses a minimal approach to highlight select antique and modern furnishings. A modern London house composed largely of concrete and glass takes its minimal tendencies seriously (opposite). The few furnishings consist of a pendant stove, Michel Ducaroy-style sofa, low table and armchairs. The visible formwork on the concrete walls becomes a key element in a room with few furnishings whose main focus is a vast window wall (not pictured) that brings light into the depths of the interior.

A minimal approach is not always an end in itself; sometimes it serves a greater purpose in giving space to other design imperatives. Previous pages: the house of a London architect features sculptural furnishings and spaces conceived to better display and give attention to the prominent works of art (left); a textured wall, and the flood of natural light, are allowed to take precedence when the rest of the decor is spare and low-key (right, top and bottom). These pages: the surrounding jungle of this Brazilian house (left) is its main decorative feature, along with the large glass and expanses of natural wood. The kitchen area is a clean-lined and unobtrusive pocket of function. The weekend island retreat of a family based in Sydney (opposite) keeps to a pure, simple aesthetic inside and out. A Serge Mouille-style wall lamp is one of the few decorative flourishes.

retro

Retro celebrates everything from the postwar 'boom' years and the birth of new 'space-age' designs and patterning to the quirky extravagances of the 1970s. In these California homes the style reflects both the vintage of the bungalow-style houses and the personal tastes of the residents. A 1950s house by Modernist builder/designer Joseph Eichler (opposite) features furnishings and objects such as the multicoloured 'ball clock' by George Nelson (1948), an Eames RAR rocker made of fibreglass-reinforced plastic (1950) and Sori Yanagi's 'butterfly' stool (1954). Deep colour on the walls and polished wood floor (above) create a subdued modern setting for a selection of retro pieces such as the amber-hued wood side tables, olive-coloured pouf and vivid turquoise ball lamp. Following pages: pieces of Scandinavian modern design and accents in tiling, lamps, dining chairs and wood veneer panelling mix happily with subtle ethnic pieces and contemporary elements while keeping to a retro scheme.

Unlike a museum arrangement, a retro interior is necessarily a mix of styles. The trick is to create a calm balance of colours, materials and patterns. This 1920s, Spanish-style Californian house (opposite and above) has become home to a collection of furnishings from the mid to late 20th century, as well as contemporary artworks and objects. Light oak floors and neutral matte-finished walls make a welcoming, calm background for furnishings in vivid colours. Wood-framed sofas and chairs with chunky upholstered cushions recall an earlier era of craft and design.

modern eclectic

Where the prevailing theme is modern but other elements and styles make their own contribution, a cool eclecticism is achieved. As in all modern schemes, a good sense of space, natural light, balance and proportion is essential. A New York apartment (above) mixes classic modern designs, such as the Eames lounge chair and Barcelona day bed, with edgy contemporary pieces in a serene, light-filled loft. Opposite, clockwise from top left: Scandinavian simplicity pervades a Danish house where a modular sofa

and rattan daybed sit beneath an ornate ceiling lamp and alongside bold graphic art; sculptural and comfortable modern furnishings meet a screen of natural wood; a modern Danish interior includes an Eames bucket chair, contemporary chandelier and large-scale artwork in the light-filled dining area; a cool, light California space with modern sectionals in bold colours. Following pages: a mix of modern minimal with other periods and patterns in California (left) and England (right).

new ethnic

There is nothing new about displaying art and objects from exotic places and cultures, but applying a more modern sensibility means that the character and features of carved wood sculpture or traditional ethnic prints will have much more resonance and appeal. Woven wood matting, carved panels and traditional louvred shutters become more than just background points in the context of a simple modern

aesthetic (opposite). The woven bamboo on the walls and ceiling (above, left) and the clay floor tiles give the impression of a tropical hideaway in this suburban California house. Rough wood beams and traditional carved-wood furnishings stand out against the simpler styling of a modern sofa (above, right). A double-height reach and skylight ensure ample doses of natural light enter the space.

mid-century modern

The period has inspired armies of enthusiasts, who continue to be fascinated by the design genius of figures such as George Nelson, Charles and Ray Eames, Mies van der Rohe, Eero Saarinen, Harry Bertoia, Florence Knoll, Isamu Noguchi, Jean Prouvé, Arne Jacobsen and Verner Panton, among others. Even Marcel Breuer and Le Corbusier, who produced their landmark furnishings in the 1920s and 1930s, are sometimes considered in the mid-century pantheon because so much of their work directly influenced the next decades. A George Nelson 'bubble' lamp and Arne Jacobsen Series 7 chairs share space with retro-style platform seating and table combinations in a California Modernist bungalow (above, left). Another 1950s house (above, right) keeps to its mid-century origins with wood veneer panelling, sliding doors and ceiling lamp. A Barcelona chair and 1950s-style dining chairs and table feature in another open-plan house (opposite).

A Danish tribute to mid-century style (opposite) includes side chairs with 'Eiffel' base designed by Charles and Ray Eames in 1948. These moulded plastic chairs, along with the Eames armchairs, were the first plastic chairs ever to be mass produced. Many of the rough stone interior walls (above) that became a trademark of 1950s and 1960s suburban houses were destroyed and covered over in subsequent decades. A restored wall now makes a stunning period backdrop for a collection of mid-century and vintage furniture. An 'egg' chair by Arne Jacobsen is covered in the 'pony hide' fabric popular at the time. The leather-covered day bed and Serge Mouille-style 'spider' sconce carry on the mid-century theme.

style baroque

baroque

A modern interior is all about flexibility. Against a carefully chosen background of solid planes in sophisticated colours and/or materials, a few flourishes can lift a room from being merely comfortably subdued to something stylishly spectacular. In a plush Brazilian apartment (opposite) a luxurious bathroom experience is achieved with the glossy reflective surfaces of glass block, a mirror wall and polished marble floor. The scalloped pedestal sink and pair of Empire-style chandeliers add a splash of grandeur. In a low-lying modern house (right), simple furnishings, including a weathered wood table, contrast with plush elements such as the high-back wing chair and downy white rug. The dark-painted side wall and fully glazed end wall bestow the modern sense of light and colour.

More baroque touches (left) in a silk-covered chair against a deep blue wall, some scrolled iron chairs and glass-topped table set on a wood-plank floor, a Venetian chandelier and 19th-century style armchair against dark walls and a period chair and ottoman against a lean white space. A plain pouf and side cabinet and unadorned walls (opposite) provide a simple framework for the crystal candlestick chandelier, classical-style bust and playful globe-based table lamps in this New Zealand apartment.

architecture

Architecture is the beginning of the home environment. A modern interior doesn't have to exist in a modern house. But the structure of the building as it affects the light, space and outdoor areas has a huge impact on how the interior can be configured and remade. Here are examples of how architecture, what many people associate with the outside of a building, gives dimension and context to living space.

hallway
84

open plan
86

opening
90

partition
92

inside out
96

double height
102

levels
108

overhang
110

balcony
112

Any book that includes some of the world's most stunning interiors will always celebrate the architecture that allows those interiors to be created. We have chosen some specific architectural features that help to create atmosphere and these are well represented in the following pages, with an array of treatments for each one.

In smaller interiors, individual areas such as hallways and balconies have much greater potential for creative thinking than you might consider possible. A long corridor can be left as a simple passage, or cleverly lined with bookcases; a balcony at the front of the house makes for a public seating area, while a rear structure can be set to overlook other parts of the private outdoor space, such as a pool or even a raised garden.

Open-plan living has become a byword for modern design. But all open-plan houses are not the same. They are not always houses, for a start. The echoing loft space of the 1980s and 1990s has given way to a far more sophisticated arrangement that looks less industrial and more home-like, while still retaining the free-flowing effect of light and movement that made open-plan spaces conjure up the image of a glamorous, bohemian existence. Open-plan areas used for bedrooms and bathrooms are less common and not to everyone's taste, but they can offer possible alternatives to traditional room designs that are worth exploring.

Openings within the house or apartment, which lead either to other rooms or to the outdoors, are another architectural element that defines the interior space. Though we have grown accustomed to squared doorways in Western architecture, Eastern cultures have long used internal arches constructed in brick or stone. Arched or rounded openings add to the drama and intimacy of the interior, pulling the senses inward, while a spacious opening to the outdoors is the best way to create a truly indoor–outdoor feeling in a house or apartment.

Another way of defining areas within the house without fully enclosing them is to use partition walls, or built-in cupboards or bookcases that function as partitions. By leaving open space above and around the partition, the flow of light (and conversation) is still free. A partition that is not used as storage can be highlighted in a vivid colour or particular material

that makes it a decorative feature as well as a functional element.

Inside out is a lifestyle concept strongly associated with warm climates, which at the forefront of the International Style that flourished in the mid-20th century in Europe and California. The International Style encouraged the creation of outdoor rooms and a form of architecture that embraced external space through the use of expanded door and window openings and the generous use of glass. These days it is much easier to find thermally efficient, strengthened glass and so the possibilities of implementing a design with oversized glass elements is much greater than when the style was first conceived. Living inside out also involves making the surrounding outdoor space connect in some way to the interior, using plantings up close to the windows and doors, which are visible from inside, and comfortable spaces outside for relaxing and entertaining that are easily accessible.

Like an open-plan space, double-height rooms allow better air and light circulation. They also add a sense of grandeur. Double-height rooms as part of an open-plan interior might also contain galleried or mezzanine spaces that encourage a more communal living experience. Sometimes these rooms are faced with one or more glass walls, opening the interior more fully to light and creating an atrium effect. Different materials might be used to mark levels without capping the ceiling, or screens, shades and light partitions can help to create semi-enclosed areas around a soaring interior space.

A house of different levels poses something of a design challenge but also provides an opportunity to create dramatic interiors. Where a living area is only a step or two below the main circulation spaces, or where rooms are set only a half-level above and stairs are open, the potential for different views through windows and rooms is greatly expanded. Materials used in these spaces need to mesh and complement each other, as sightlines move around and through the architecture.

An extended or cantilevered roof also encourages the movement of activities between indoors and out. Used with large glass doors or fully opening shutters, an overhang can make the interior and the terrace area feel, and be used, like one free-flowing space.

hallway

The hallway is necessarily a utilitarian space. It provides transition between rooms and from indoors to out, and it can be a good place for facilitating storage. But the hallway as a confined and sterile corridor is history. Even a narrow functional traffic conduit can be livened up with a prominent object or source of light. Refurbishment of an old farmhouse and outbuildings in Provence, France (left), brings more light and modern proportions to an entrance hall. Here the shadows of the glazing bars cast a dynamic pattern on the bare stone walls. Opposite, clockwise from top left: louvred shutters and window benches make a hallway a place for relaxation in a Sri Lankan house; a hallway that follows the external wall of a 1926 house by the architect Lloyd Wright in Los Angeles is lined with carved wood panels that allow light to permeate the internal spaces; an open mezzanine becomes a display space for an antique bench and modern painting; the hallway becomes a haven for a variety of inventive storage solutions.

open plan

Open plan has become a cliché of modern living. But the freedom and flexibility it allows within a house or apartment mean that open-plan spaces are here to stay. A lack of walls does not mean a lack of comfort or order. In a single open space, where natural light permeates everywhere, furniture groupings offer the only references to separate functional areas. This house in São Paulo, Brazil (right), features the ultimate open-plan interior. The free-flowing ground-floor living and dining area is mirrored by the space on the open mezzanine above. Bookshelves and storage on both levels emphasize the double-height reach of the interior and make the entire space read as one airy volume. Areas of interest or relaxation are marked out using furniture, art and objects, such as the 'tulip' chairs and dining table by Eero Saarinen at one side, and the sofa and bench at left.

An open-plan arrangement might also include partitions and areas enclosed on three sides, as in this New York loft apartment (opposite, top), an airy white space with modern furnishings. Fashion designer Donna Karan's New York apartment (opposite, bottom) is an open space

that uses partitions to articulate areas without enclosing rooms. The design includes low built-in sofas and a wall of windows overlooking the city. The upstairs rooms of an old house in Copenhagen (above) were converted for use as living space with minimal built interventions so

that the interiors retain the building's original grand proportions and form. The resulting space is arranged using rugs and furnishings to define the sitting areas. A single colour scheme is especially beneficial in smaller open-plan interiors, where functions need to overlap.

opening

Arches, circular cut-outs, cavernous vaults
and rounded openings (opposite) give
an interior immediate character with
references to building details, craftsman
style or period charm. Smaller openings
also create a sense of intimacy. But even
a standard squared door-frame can
find distinction in a wall of books or
paintings. An unusual opening, perhaps
painted in a distinctive or contrasting
colour, frames the view into another room.
This page, clockwise from top left: the
entrance to a Brazilian house is framed
in striking rusted steel; a house in
Melbourne uses dark paint to contrast
with the natural light flowing through the
rooms; a house in Los Angeles employs
two different approaches for the wall
space surrounding a doorway – a coloured
cut-out wall with a glazed section for a
door that leads to the bathroom (right),
and a wall of books (left).

partition

Following on from the open-plan arrangement, a space can be divided up using partitions instead of walls so that the flow of light and movement is still freer than in a standard interior composed of separate rooms. Partitions can be created in a number of ways, from stand-alone pieces that double up as storage to plain walls that leave a gap between the top and the ceiling. In dramatic wood, glass or other materials, the partition becomes a decorative focus rather than just a dividing plane. A mid-century house outside of Los Angeles (above, left) retains its retro feel with modern wood units that contain storage and utility space while also defining the kitchen and dining areas. A house by the Modernist-influenced developer Joseph Eichler, who was greatly inspired by the work of Frank Lloyd Wright and Mies van der Rohe (above, right), features partition walls in wood veneer of the kind favoured by Mies in some of his residential designs. A bedroom and bathroom are partially separated by an elegant section wall (opposite) in a modern house on the northeast coast of Australia.

A house overlooking Sydney Harbour (opposite) features partitions that recall delicate Japanese rice-paper screens and soften the incoming daylight. The sliding walls help the interior rooms reach out to the long wood-lined balcony and the thick greenery beyond. A series of clerestory windows in a house near Brisbane, Australia (above), lets light travel from outdoors and through the internal spaces. This view takes in almost every room of the house as the partitions and doors can be folded back to open up the whole interior. Extending materials like the gravel floor, along with the wood and glass, helps to blend the outside space with the inside.

inside out

Making a house open to the outdoors is a goal for many people living in all climates, but it is particularly successful in places where the temperature allows the spaces to be freely opened for much of the year. In a colourfully clad house in southern California (below) the floor plane is level with the outdoor paving stones, and the water of the reflecting pond gives the house the appearance of floating.

In this desert house in California (opposite), the architects made use of large areas of glass and simple planes to let the outdoor landscape become part of the house. Following pages: a suburban house that is like a natural oasis around a courtyard pool has a sunken kitchen space that is almost on level with the water, topped with a grass-covered roof.

Smaller rooms can also be turned into indoor–outdoor spaces by adding fully openable screens or sliding doors, and continuing flooring materials from inside to out, as in this house near São Paulo in Brazil (opposite). Massive glass doors can be swung open to create a grand space. A different take on bringing the outdoors in is the retractable roof on this house in old parkland in London (right). Fashion designer John Rocha's French Mediterranean retreat (below, left) is a wondrous, white composition that takes every opportunity to let in air and sunlight, while the lifting screens on this house in a Brazilian resort (below, right) act as a sun shade by day and provide protection from high winds when closed.

double height

A space that is double height feels immediately grand and luxurious, especially with natural light pouring in all around. Soaring spaces are less daunting when the levels are articulated through a change in materials or windows, and where mezzanine rooms offer glimpses of domestic activity on the levels above. In a traditional house in Sri Lanka (above, left) galleried walkways lit by shuttered windows traverse the upper level. The filtered daylight casts a warm glow through the wood structure. Rooms and features are all on display with the different levels clearly visible in a modern Australian house with white-washed interiors (above, right). Elsewhere, double-height proportions create great opportunities for bringing in natural light through a glazed wall (opposite). An assortment of window openings helps to control temperature and air flow in this light-filled house in Noosa, Australia.

Double-height interiors are not always organized as a single hall or atrium. To break up the volume while keeping the sense of space, this house on the Australian coast (opposite) has a projecting mezzanine that appears to float above the kitchen and is open to the natural light from the wall of windows. In the same house (above, right), the massive verticality of a chimney breast forms the centre of the living area, emphasizing the soaring ceiling height but also grounding and focusing the room. The wood cladding is a warm contrast to the large window walls. Decorative screens and hangings (above, left, top and bottom) help to define the upper levels in other interiors. Following pages: a modern house of wood, glass and steel is an elegant intrusion on the Brazilian forest.

levels

There is something intriguing about a house that is arranged over half-levels rather than having rooms stacked vertically or set next to each other. In rooms of more than standard height, split or stepped levels make for a beguiling interior while still allowing for the flow of natural light. Rooms that are articulated by a half-level or a few steps in one direction become semi-secluded pockets of living space. In modern, open schemes where the climate allows for large expanses of glass and light, these spaces can be fully opened to the outside or nestled within the core of the house. A suburban Australian house (opposite) offers a variety of calm open rooms with a Zen-like simplicity, using wood and opaque glass to provide areas of privacy or quiet. A platform kitchen in a London townhouse (above, left) is surprisingly light, as is a sunken kitchen in a California house overlooking a courtyard swimming pool (above, right).

overhang

A cantilever is a beam that projects from one area of support. This can be achieved with the beam anchored to the core of the building, or even into pilings in a steep hillside. The modern cantilevered building not only creates spaces that reach out into the trees or open air, it adds sheltered outdoor areas below for entertaining or relaxing. A simple roof overhang can perform the same function, protecting glazed walls from the strongest sunlight while covering a portion of the terrace and making it into an 'outdoor room'. Two hillside houses by the futuristic Modernist John Lautner (above) extend beyond the slope so that the main living spaces are floating in the tree canopy. A house on pilings (opposite) affords two levels of sheltered outdoor space: one beneath the main house and another created by the extension of the roof and wall planes.

balcony

Whether it is a space only large enough for a café table and chair and a few potted plants, or a capacious terrace that is perfect for alfresco dining, a balcony is a precious amenity, particularly in dense urban sites. John Lautner's design (left), which has recently been renovated and updated, retains its thoroughly modern style with balconies open to the clear California skies. The balcony spaces are sheltered by the mass of the house and the hill but the transparent walls allow for views through the living space to the hills beyond. Following pages: two more external views from Lautner's California house; the balcony of a glass house overlooks Highgate Cemetery in London; a treehouse has its own balcony, where designer Todd Oldham retreats to a child-like hiding place in the trees; and a wood-clad house in Singapore sits like a houseboat with balconies hovering over the water's edge.

materials

The materials of construction underline the fundamental character of a house. A rustic stone cottage, a free-form futuristic concrete bunker, a sprawling, marble-lined villa or a wood-panelled townhouse all communicate a sense of place and attitude from the mere substance of their walls, roof and floors. Add to this the products used for cabinets, doors, screens and stairs, and the material of a house begins to have more presence than just a background surface. Stone, tile, glass, wood, metal, brick, woven and mixed elements help define the way a house looks, feels and even how it functions.

wood
122

concrete
128

glass
130

marble
136

metal
138

mixed
140

natural
142

brick & stone
144

People can have an almost visceral reaction to materials. Wood implies warmth. Concrete, glass and steel are cold. Brick and stone can also be cold, but a stone cottage with a nice fire says cosy, rather than draughty, and has an integrity that people associate with what are often called 'honest materials': those that have not been manufactured or alloyed. In a world where we are aware of the scarcity of natural resources, materials have become a more considered part of buildings and interiors. Wood has the advantage of being a natural material but we may be concerned with whether it has come from a managed forest, been sustainably harvested or whether it represents an endangered species.

Another environmental consideration is how efficiently certain materials insulate a house against extreme temperatures or conditions. Advances in glass manufacture mean that large expanses of wall or roof can be covered in glass that is as thermally efficient as concrete or brick, but obviously better at bringing natural light, a view, and some heat gain inside. Concrete is often used in warmer climates because it absorbs heat. Some areas also have strong traditions of using specific building materials. Wood has long been employed in certain parts of Europe but not so much in Britain; however, that is changing. Nowadays there is a greater flexibility in the use of all materials due to awareness of global styles and methods, and also as a result of advanced technologies in insulation and energy efficiency. Decisions about use are increasingly aesthetic.

Without tradition or location to dictate which materials we use, we come back to the way a material 'feels' in both the tactile and the emotional senses. And we have to admit certain assumptions. We might perceive it as a given that a cabin will be made of wood, a townhouse will be brick, a cottage will be stone. A room with large windows framed in concrete or steel feels very different from one made of timber planks, though both allow for an enormous amount of natural light and generous views. One is still more 'homely' than the other. But even if we do not want to diverge from these attitudes, it is still possible to have a new experience with materials.

Sometimes the most interesting trait of a house is the way the material is used. There are different treatments that make almost any material fit with widely different environments. Wood has enormous variation in texture, finish and method. A wood plank floor is friendly and rustic, highly suitable for a rural

dwelling, whereas a floor of highly polished inlay or hardwood looks stunning in a sophisticated modern house or apartment. Smooth, built-in wood cabinetry has a very modern edge, while other wood furnishings might be scrolled antiques, rough-hewn pieces or high-design computer-generated forms. A rough concrete wall or one that shows the visible marks of formwork has an entirely different feel to a polished concrete floor, which has some of the sheen and variation of marble. So the choice of material is not always limiting. An interior that combines different textures of even a single material provides layers of visual and tactile experience.

This is also true of combined materials. A house using concrete formwork alongside steel and glass allows the properties of each to stand out in contrast to the others. The imperfections of concrete take on the warmth of hand-crafted material against peerless glass, while the brute strength of steel balances the apparent fragility of a window wall. A slab of marble next to a slatted wood cladding wall reveals the natural patterning and burls in each.

And it is not only the building materials in a house that contribute to its effect. Furniture and decorative objects can make a marked contrast or a smooth complement to the fabric of the walls and floors. A modern glass table against an old stone floor makes us look at each with fresh appreciation. A formal glass chandelier against a natural woven ceiling mat is both charming and pleasantly quirky. A solid stone or brick wall has its own texture and variation, but it can also become a three-dimensional canvas for brighter objects. The hard surface quality and colour of brick and stone are subdued alongside soft furnishings and rugs or sharpened against plush fabrics.

Going back to Mies van der Rohe's Barcelona Pavilion, we can see how his choices of glass, rust-coloured onyx, pale travertine and green Tinian marbles were not lessons in stark purity so much as in the appreciation of the finer qualities of the materials. That appreciation also takes in the natural variation, which is as appealing in a cool modern environment as in a more casual setting. Stone, wood, concrete, even metal show grain, weathering and discolouration that demonstrate the beauty of a natural process, and have an enduring quality that translates a sense of solidity to the living space and offers comfort in a sense of history and durability.

wood

Wood is probably the most versatile and changeable building material. Used for millennia, it is most often described as bringing a feeling of warmth to a room. With the careful sourcing of wood from sustainable forests, there is a remarkable variety of hard and soft woods that can be used without causing unnecessary damage to rare species or the ecosystem. From the rustic farmhouse to glamorous city apartment, wood is an infinitely adaptable and endlessly fascinating addition to the modern interior. A newly refurbished farmhouse in Chile (opposite) pairs modern fixtures, furnishings and design with natural wood beams, planked floors, panels and window frames. A modern British house (above, left) makes use of a more refined surface quality. In the Danish countryside (above, right) the Scandinavian taste for pure wood finishes in a modern context is apparent.

Previous pages, left: the many faces and variations of wood – from weathered shingles and clapboard siding to luxurious decking, sophisticated panelling and modern veneers – attest to the infinite possibilities of a humble material. Previous pages, right: variations of finish and method in a clean-lined modern house in Australia. These pages: a Singapore house mixes hardwood with lots of glass and concrete. The natural woven rug mediates the sharpness of the other materials against the rich wood elements.

concrete

It has been used since ancient times, but nowadays concrete is almost immediately associated with modern building, particularly with some of the more maligned housing experiments of the 1950s and 1960s. Yet concrete is a versatile material that can be full of variation and character. It can also be relatively inexpensive to use and is capable of being recycled and reused in different amalgamations. Concrete coupled with dark hardwood (above, left) creates an elegant, sophisticated interior background in a modern New Zealand house. Aided by natural light, the slender metal elements of stairs used with open stair risers (above, right) give a surprisingly delicate feeling to the concrete elements. Using any material in different textures or forms will create a richer interior composition (opposite). Here a highly polished concrete floor contrasts with the rougher walls and ceiling. Juxtaposing planes of different materials also adds a sense of dynamism.

glass

If Modernism is about using the most advanced materials available as efficiently as possible, then glass has to be a thoroughly modern material. Even in the decades since the modern movement popularized the use of large panes of unobstructed glass, developments in thermal technology and structural toughening mean that, though it still feels as luxurious as ever to have massive glazed panels in the home, nowadays we can do this without sacrificing practicality. A house in Singapore (opposite) juxtaposes discrete steel elements with glass in interesting geometries. The glass-panelled stair lets natural light flow from above the stairwell through to the ground-floor dining area. An open-plan house in California (above) creates a transition between the interior and the outdoors with pivoting steel-framed glass walls. When opened they create a series of sculptural elements. Following pages: unframed glass changes character when used with wood, steel and concrete.

materials glass

marble

Marble has enchanted and delighted people for millennia. From the ethereal beauty of pure limestone to the swirling patterns caused by mineral impurities, marble is not just a convenient material for a wet area but also an object of subtle natural beauty. Treatments include stand-alone panels against wood or other materials that bring out the variations in each (below, left, top); the luxurious use of a single large panel to line a shower area (below, right); or and an inset shelf (below, left, bottom). Overlapping slabs of marble form a countertop that appears to float over the base (opposite). The silvery veins running through the white stone complement the striking wood grain on the cupboards and panelling.

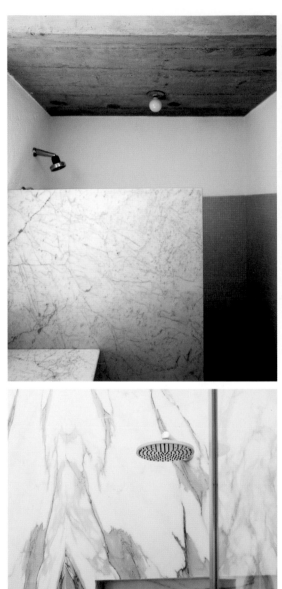

metal

People started to become used to the presence of visible steel beams in domestic buildings with the steel-and-glass constructions of the International Style houses of the 1920s and 1930s. Steel beams are still a part of most houses that boast large glass window walls. Developed at the beginning of the 20th century, stainless steel became popular for architectural cladding – the St Louis Arch and the Chrysler Building are two US landmarks that are covered in it. Stainless steel was the material of choice for design-conscious kitchens at the beginning of the 21st century. Its non-corrosive, allergen-resistant properties make it well suited for use in the kitchen, and its polished surface speaks of cleanliness and modern efficiency. It can also look sophisticated while being very utilitarian, as in this house in Los Angeles (opposite). In a contemporary British house (right) a dramatic curved aluminium desk, designed in 1971 by Nino Cecci, creates a sculptural contrast in a room of sharp right angles and planked wood floors.

mixed

As the modern movement called on designers and builders to make the best use of the most advanced materials, the efficiency and beauty of one material versus another became part of an ongoing dialogue that played out in the new housing styles of the period. This house by Mies van der Rohe (above, left) is a symbol of modern simplicity. The bathroom, a later addition to the house, uses a striking mix of materials in its stepped planes: frosted glass, steel, tile and marble. The ornament is all in the surface patterns, textures and reflections. A New Zealand house

(above, right) mixes polished concrete, concrete brick and hardwood in a room of clean intersecting planes. This house in Los Angeles (opposite, left) is a palette of hard materials that might be used on an exterior. The pebble-surface concrete is interrupted by a mezzanine marked out by clapboard cladding. Steel beams frame large glass sliding doors and the granite floor is impervious to water or debris from outside. Elsewhere, the silvery sheen and variegated tones of weathered antique wood blend with modern decking and neat stone walls in Bali (opposite, right).

natural

Most materials used in house construction are
somehow formed of natural elements. But it is
the unprocessed, raw character of woven fibres,
pole or bamboo constructions that make a
satisfying connection to the natural environment.
Juxtaposing these with more refined objects,
such as the modern glass pendant light
(opposite, top right), makes vibrant contrasts
and calls attention to the natural versus man-
made qualities and patterns. A California house
(opposite, bottom left) references native
American adobe and lodgepole structures using
bamboo segments to create a box shade for
a window on an exposed façade. Elsewhere,

bamboo and moss line an outdoor garden space,
and designer Todd Oldham makes his treehouse
ladder from the real thing. The quiet
sophistication of the cool modern poolside in
this Brazilian house (above, left) is enhanced by
the massive patterned volume of the stone slab
that was allowed to project through the floor
area from the ground below, while a desert
boulder was deliberately incorporated into this
hillside house in a canyon above Palm Springs,
California (above, right), designed by the
Modernist architect Albert Frey in the early
1960s. Walls of glass further emphasize the link
to the desert landscape.

brick & stone

Stone is a naturally coloured and varied material that brings its own solid rustic character to an interior. This 1950s house in California (opposite, left) is an example of the popular taste for undressed stone walls in so-called 'ranch-style' suburban houses of the period. It is appropriately paired with furnishings such as this Arne Jacobsen 'egg' chair upholstered in a 'pony hide' pattern and the long shag pile rug. When English townhouses such as this (opposite, right) were built in the 19th century, the interior brick was usually covered in render. This exposed, re-pointed and sealed wall now presents a modern sense of pride in its revealed structure, giving the entrance a rich, warm period feel. The earthiness of thinly sliced stone and dark wood is countered by the highly polished floor of this sophisticated Australian design (above, left), while another Australian house makes a feature of a monumental chimney breast in irregular cut stone (above, right). Following pages: a wall of massive stone slabs in a Balinese garden is softly coloured by moss; another British townhouse uses exposed brick to contrast with modern furnishings and spaces; rough stone contrasts with plush fabrics and smooth surfaces; undressed stone in a French chateau can take almost any decorative style.

surface

Rough or smooth, weathered, polished, glossy or matte, the form and texture of interior surfaces convey subtle messages about style, ambience, even about place and function. The qualities of natural wood or hand-crafted tile, concrete formwork or gleaming enamel establish underlying themes of the decor that support or set up a creative contrast with other elements, such as furnishings and decorative objects. Whether it is hardwood flooring, painted walls or a ceiling pattern, the surfaces set the scene and the mood for the modern interior.

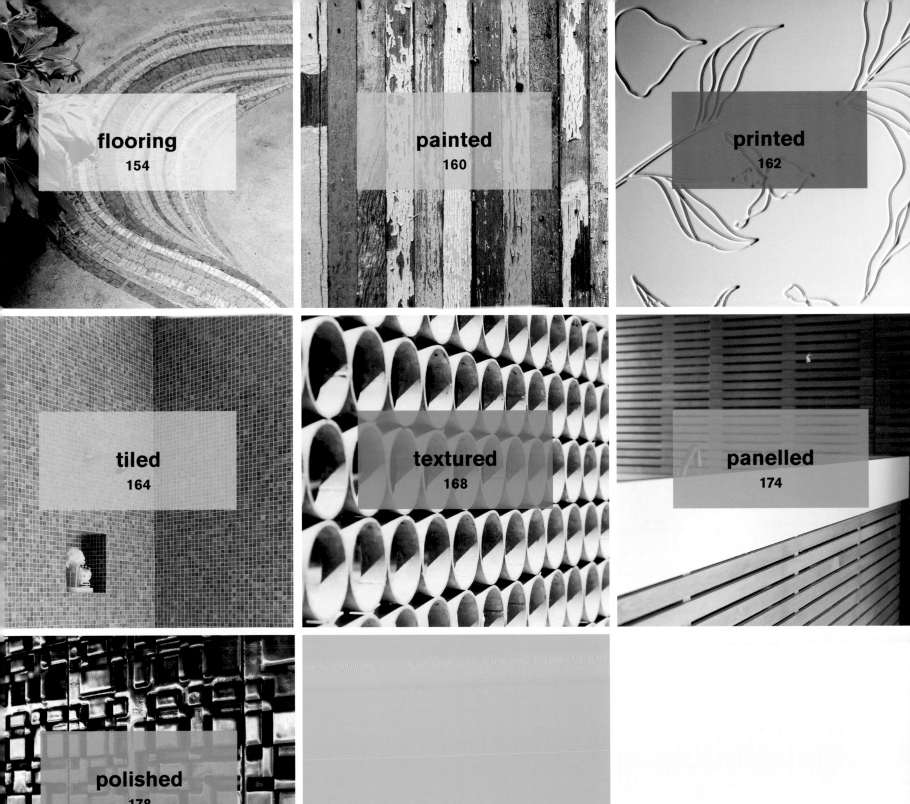

flooring
154

painted
160

printed
162

tiled
164

textured
168

panelled
174

polished
178

If Modernism could be said to have had a single lasting influence, it might be the appreciation of materials. And nowhere is the quality of material more prominent than in wall, floor and ceiling surfaces. These large measures of space allow the most fascinating characteristics of wood, tile, concrete, stone or marble to be revealed. The most successful interiors will keep the number of surface materials to a precious few. But these few will provide an opportunity to enhance the atmosphere with greater impact than possibly any other single element, except perhaps the amount of natural light, on a room or interior as a whole.

When the word 'surfaces' is mentioned, people often think of cabinets and countertops, and while these are areas where we often come into contact with the actual material of the building, there are also the surrounding surfaces that are the background to every piece of furniture or artwork, framing windows and doorways and creating partitions. Many still assume that a modern interior will consist of sprawling white rectangular planes, but as we have shown, that vision of pure Minimalism is one small aspect of the modern interior. All manner of surface materials can be part of a modern vision as long as they are allowed to have a certain amount of integrity.

Surface materials matter to modern design as they have not in the past. The Romans revelled in trompe l'oeil and invented concrete. Medieval house interiors were to a large extent determined by the size and use of wood and stone. Baroque decor reproduced just about any material, marble, stone or gold, through the careful work of master decorative painters. The Regency period rediscovered Classical elements, such as pilasters and cornices, and a palette of colours that suited the Neoclassical theme. The Victorians had a love affair with wallpaper and, in the UK at least, with deeper hues than their predecessors would have chosen. However, these decorative tastes were mostly applied over plaster or wood. During the Arts and Crafts period at the end of the 19th century, an appreciation of wood as a material to be worked and appreciated on its own came to the fore, as did the possibilities of decorative glass. Though there have always been interior masterworks of particular materials, it was the Modernists who focused so intently on the beauty and character of surface materials.

Though today's modern interiors do not necessarily concentrate on surfaces at the cost of all other furnishings, they do show a greater awareness of surface qualities and finishes than in the past. To begin with, flooring is more an integral part of an interior than it once was. A wood floor of fine parquetry was always a luxury and something to be admired, in a ballroom, perhaps. But nowadays a plank wood floor might be just as admired and refined, whether in exotic hardwood or reclaimed pine boards. As we become more aware of allergens and other pollutants, hard floors of other materials are increasingly popular. Stone or clay tile, polished concrete and other forms of marble or granite are also naturally beautiful substances in their own right.

Painted surfaces mostly refer to wall colour, though floors and ceilings of course could be included here too. And though there is nothing particularly modern about a painted wall, the style of painting and the pigments determine whether it appears as something of the present moment or of the past. Modern rooms with a careful balance of decorative treatments can take deeper and more daring colours and still feel balanced. Similarly, printed walls or wall-coverings are nothing new, but it is the way they are used, and the combinations in which they are used, that mark out the rooms shown here as particularly modern.

Tiles are as old as houses and it seems likely that even the most hardened purist will find a type of tile to embrace, whether for a small bathroom corner or a dining-room wall. Texture, also, is hard not to enjoy in some way, whether it is unfinished concrete or highly polished wood. Usually it is the variations that give character and dimension to a room. Beginning with the main surface texture, the other objects and furnishings can be used to contrast or layer different tactile experiences.

Panelled surfaces are not the cheap wall veneers of previous decades, but the artful use of sections to create patterns, to frame windows and, yes, to conceal storage and other functional necessities behind planes of a more pleasing or luxurious material. And few things seem more luxurious than large polished surfaces, not merely clinical spaces but lustrous walls or floors that are not only reflective but also rich to behold, even in white, and tempting to touch, despite the fear of fingerprints. For all surfaces should invite close examination, to inspire appreciation and provide lasting appeal.

flooring

Choice of flooring is always a practical as well as a decorative decision. Even then, there is a surprising range of materials and treatments to consider for all climates and styles. The indoor–outdoor nature of this Brazilian kitchen and patio (below, left) is enhanced by the even floor level on both sides of the threshold. Different materials are used but they are equally robust. A modern house in Sri Lanka with traditional features (below, right) retains the aged clay floor tiles, which complement both the new and old elements.

The natural variations of the planks in this hardwood floor (left) add colour and character to an otherwise spare interior. Below, from left: an Australian house with a taste for tiles creates a nostalgic feel with a chequerboard floor; a stark modern interior uses polished concrete to follow the bold curving shapes throughout; a stamped pattern floor in Sri Lanka echoes the patterning of a set of modern iconic Barcelona chairs.

Modern flooring in concrete, granite and glass. In a new-build London house (opposite), concrete walls showing the patterns of formwork contrast with the smooth glow of a glass floor panel. Positioned over the stair, a series of these glazed panels allow light to travel through the house. A low, open-style retreat in Brazil (above, left) has a generous, shaded poolside terrace. The rough granite floor surface is balanced and softened by the natural wood ceiling treatment. In an artist's São Paulo house (above, right), concrete walls and floor provide a neutral showcase for large, colourful artworks and objects, while an abstract shape in mosaic brings colour and movement to a small British garden space (left). Following pages: a cool, minimal house uses glass partitions and a polished white floor to reflect natural light (left); the glossy, reflective floor of this New York apartment provides an edgy backdrop for classic modern furnishings and massive artworks (right).

painted

Painting walls and ceilings is as common in modern houses as in any other style of home, but the modern approach takes into account variations in texture and more subtle colours. Sophisticated tones are achieved using a large number of mix colours and result in a richer hue, whether light or dark. The residents of a California house (left) with a penchant for retro-style objects and furniture have chosen a turquoise wall colour that is reminiscent of the postwar period, but this one has a fresh modern tone. The stair rail adds another hint of retro style and a lively pattern to the colour. Opposite, clockwise from top left: an alluring deep blue-black wall makes a dramatic setting for the dining area of Donna Karan's New York apartment; painted wall and ceiling boards update a California house; rough stucco walls are enriched with a deep gold tone; multi-coloured wood cladding looks appealing even when in a weathered condition; a restored Italian hilltop villa takes a striped, duotone wall colour; a bold contrast of colours gives a fresh modern atmosphere to an old French farmhouse.

printed

Printed wall-covering, like paint, is a familiar decorative treatment that has a different appeal in the modern context. Going back to the idea of balance, it is easy to see how some rooms with printed surfaces are part of an old-fashioned composition that might include layers of pattern, colour and texture, while others carry a more modern arrangement where plain surfaces and simple objects provide a serene framework for the colour and pattern of a printed surface.

A renovated French villa (above) was given a high modern interior with a glamorous theme of dark and light contrast. The printed wallpaper panel adds both texture and dynamism to the sedate dining space. A bolder approach to pattern in this California house (opposite) still retains a cool modern sensibility. The daring wallpaper illustration was created by the resident, a graphic designer, and is tempered by solid surfaces; the chandelier is balanced with Eames-style dining chairs.

tiled

Tiles possess the allure of being both pleasingly tactile and highly practical. The range of tiles, from tiny uniform mosaics to handmade pieces in distempered colours, offers almost unlimited possibilities for uses and styles. Classic Metro tiles, which were first used in the Paris underground, have a brick shape and bevelled edge. This 19th-century London townhouse (left) uses a version of the Metro tile throughout, unifying the rooms as a continuous space. There is an unlikely but intriguing use of a similar tile design in the dining room of this Turkish apartment (opposite), where period elements such as the decorative ceiling rose contrast with modern objects like the constellation chandelier. Following pages: tile treatments that range from cool elegance, to subtly patterned, to retro and funky.

textured

Texture keeps a space feeling rich and lively and can be achieved with hard surfaces as well as soft furnishings. Almost any surface will contribute some kind of textural influence to the interior design, whether as a single element or in opposition to other materials. Opposite, clockwise from top left: contrasts in tone and texture in a California house with a rough stucco wall and coloured shutter; wood shingle on a Long Island holiday home; uniform concrete brick in a New Zealand entryway; rough stucco up against Singaporean greenery. The natural roughness of a concrete stair wall in a rammed-earth house in Austria (right) emphasizes the earthy materials of the building. The beauty of old stone (below, right) and formwork concrete (below, left).

Contrasting unfinished concrete with rough wood (left) brings out the distinctive qualities of each in the poolside eating area of a Brazilian retreat. Opposite, clockwise from top left: a mesh curtain, a woven leather chair, textured tiles and pleated draperies add pattern as well as texture to the interior; wood has a rustic feel and character in the Blue Mountains cabin of Australian fashion designer Jenny Kee, where the natural shape and wear of log construction is balanced by the smooth planked floors; the natural grain of smooth solid wood is used in clean modern panes in a Florida retreat; handmade glazed tiles by Heath Ceramics in San Francisco add warm colour and texture to a kitchen workspace. Following pages: a colour-tinted concrete wall and a smooth sandy finish have their own natural variations in texture and tone.

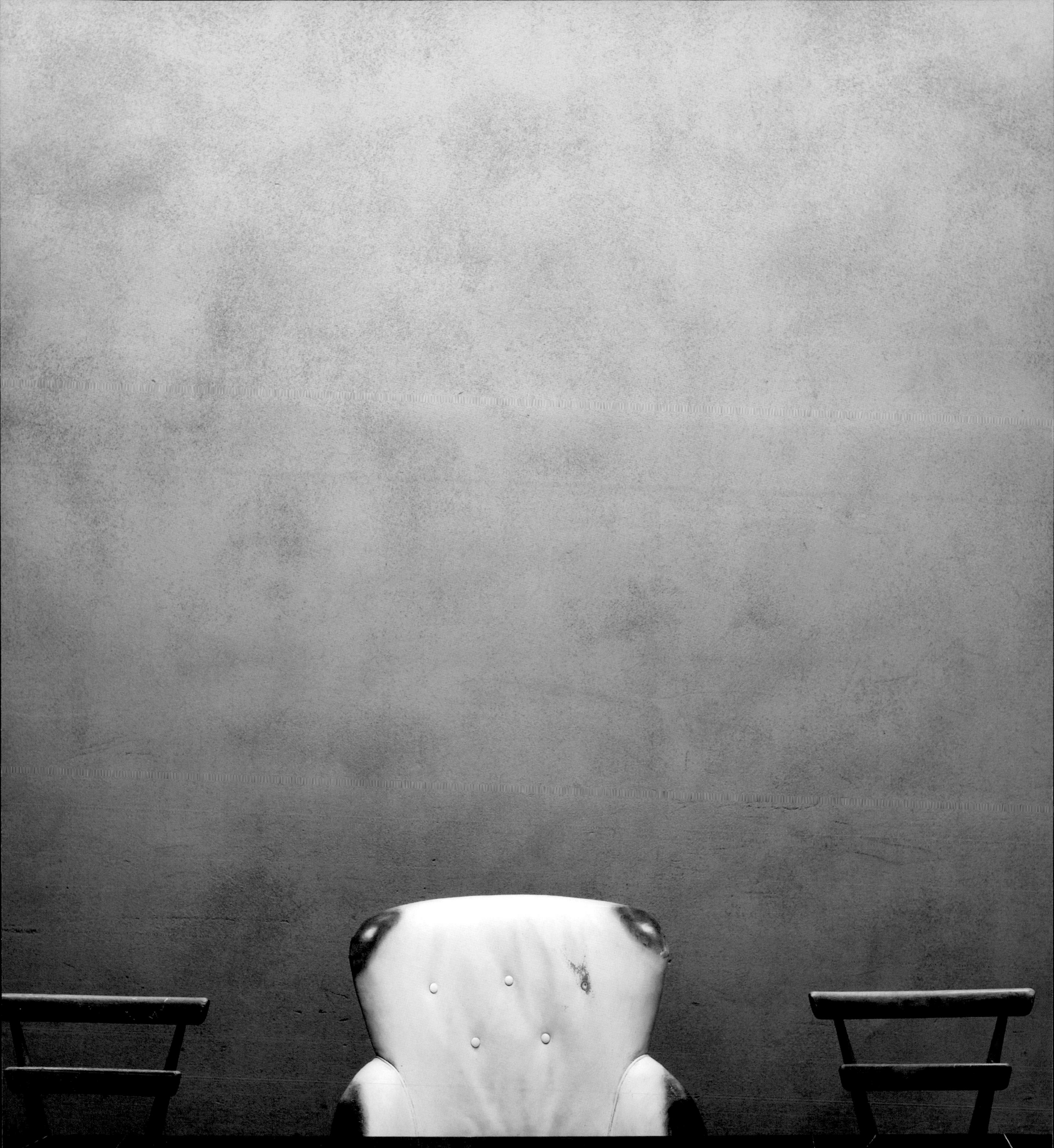

panelled

Panels or sections create pattern and texture, whether in the same material or by using contrasting elements. A British riverside retreat (opposite, left) uses sections of slim-planked wall panelling, wide-plank floors and pure white planes to echo the wooded surroundings while keeping a clean modern aspect. A Danish house outside Copenhagen (opposite, right) filled with avant-garde art and materials boasts a modern exterior that retains the traditional wood cladding but in a fine beaded adaptation. Another modern take on wood cladding can be seen in this house in Brazil (above, left), where sections of white-painted trellised board cover the top portion of the house with openable panels that shade or cover the windows. More innovative exterior cladding in panelled sections gives an intriguing geometric variation to a suburban house in Los Angeles (above, right). The sections of dark board alternate with window openings framed in bright green and white-washed stucco. Following pages: panelling in a more traditional style in a French apartment is given an updating treatment of colour and contrast (left). In a room of spare decor and solid colour, the details of the woodwork become more appreciable. Panels made of beech ply create a patterned effect on the walls and ceiling of a modern Danish cottage (right).

polished

The polished interior is often thought of as projecting a more glamorous atmosphere than textured environments. Natural and artificial light also play a part in highlighting or softening a glossy surface. There is certainly high style in evidence in this California residence (above, left) in which pattern and colour in other areas of the house have been tamed to create a dark, polished drama in the dining area. The brooding elegance of dark wood and mirrors carries a theme of modern art and new-century technology in a London apartment (above, right). In the cool white interiors of a Dubai desert house (opposite, left), even subtle differences in texture resonate, such as the distinction between plaster and concrete. Here, polished marble slabs on the stairs are a sleek intervention in both colour and surface quality. The high polish of wood, glass and enamel can be countered by books and soft furnishings (opposite, right).

function

While rooms in the modern sense are versatile spaces, they still need to cater for the basic activities that we need in a home: cooking, eating, bathing, relaxing, sleeping, working, entertaining. Even the entrance to a house can be made to reflect a particular personality and atmosphere. However, function means different things to different people, and it should be considered in a variety of contexts as there are exciting possibilities for making each space a delight.

entering
186

living
188

cooking & eating
194

entertaining
202

working
206

sleeping
208

bathing
212

In the current century we are accustomed to thinking of rooms according to function. But it was not always so. In the Middle Ages in Europe most townhouses consisted of a single hall or room for cooking, eating, lounging and sleeping. Separate rooms, or 'privacies', as they were called, became more common after the 16th century, when the townhouse emerged as something more than protective shelter. As time went on people adapted to the idea of private spaces, and of separate rooms for disparate functions, however, the problem of heating meant that all of those rooms were closed off from one another to keep in the warmth.

So our modern preoccupation with open-plan living actually goes back to the original idea of a living space. Today, using one room for multiple activities makes great sense, especially if that room has a pleasant aspect, a nice view over hills, water or skyline, or a comforting amount of natural light. With improvements in heating and insulation, we can heat larger areas more efficiently and so do away with the maze of doors and hallways that were necessary to keep all of those separate rooms cosy.

Still, we might be restricted by architecture or by the desire to keep certain functions separate. But that approach also leaves vast scope for innovation, as we have the freedom to reconsider how those functions are shared or separated, no longer by necessity, but by personal preference and ease of use.

If we look at the entrance, for example, there are several ways this space serves the house. These days we often enter from the street into a vestibule of some kind, but older houses, particularly rural dwellings, might open directly into a kitchen or living space, or guests might be met by a utility area before they are ushered into the main public part of the house. These transitions are opportunities for creating an atmosphere that welcomes the visitor to enjoy the rest of the house, using natural light where possible and providing a taste of the materials and colours used elsewhere.

The living area is the next space that a visitor will experience, and often this will be open to a dining room or kitchen. Here, built-in storage or kitchen island units are useful for delineating functions without separating them completely. The living area itself might just be an inward-facing arrangement of furnishings that creates a set piece within the open-plan space. This makes entertaining fluid, especially where the indoor spaces meld with outdoors.

Kitchens are no longer the private domain of servants or hosts, but are often open in some way to the view of others in the house. As the popularity of cooking and the demand for freshly prepared foods has increased over the past decade, the space we require for kitchens has also grown. These rooms represent a celebration of cooking that is a break with the past. Our current desire for bigger, more open kitchens demonstrates our very modern appreciation of food and culinary skill.

Spaces for entertaining are also more fluid in the modern house. They can include the kitchen/dining area or a more open-plan living and dining space. A formal dining room is ripe for entertaining, but so is a dining area that is a part of the open-plan space and set apart by lighting and furniture design. In houses where the formal dining room exists it is often a treat, a room of high drama, with walls, upholstery and draperies in deep colours or textured fabrics, and candles and other forms of low-pitched lighting helping to create a sense of occasion.

Another throwback to the past is our habit of working out of the home. Office or studio spaces have become the norm not just in airy lofts and converted buildings but also in most modern houses.

But a work space does not always mean a purely functional room with a desk and bookcases. If a creative mind is to find inspiration, then these spaces need almost as much colour and character as areas for lounging or entertaining. Functional elements can be artfully mixed with more exuberant gestures, evidence that an aesthetically pleasing space is part of a healthy work/life balance.

Bedrooms have always been considered private, and in most modern houses this is still the case. But a bedroom can be open to a bathing area, overlook a fine view or include its own seating area or desk. These are choices that reinforce the ideas of comfort and versatility that are central to the modern house.

Bathrooms are also spaces of utility that have evolved and are now potentially much more luxurious. One expression of luxury is the placement of a freestanding tub outside the confines of the purpose-built tiled room. Whether next to a large window shaded only by outside greenery, or set in an open space as part of the bedroom, the bath has migrated beyond its previous limits, offering yet another example of how modern living is about transcending established boundaries.

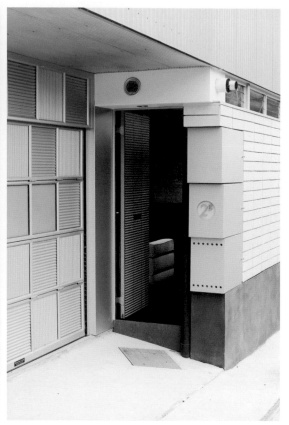

entering

Beyond the question of 'What does your entrance say about you?', the entrance says something about the rest of the house or expresses an attitude to visitors. Whether the door is set back from a garden or lawn or protected by a courtyard wall determines how open or transparent the entrance can be while still maintaining privacy. Opposite, top, from left: a suburban house keeps to a narrow opening, while another with a sheltered entry can offer a wider entrance and glazed frame; an on-street entrance to an Australian house uses a clever turn to mask the doorway from public view and street traffic. Opposite, bottom, from left: a boldly coloured California house welcomes visitors with paving stones set in a shallow pond; a Brazilian house presents a monolithic façade and an enclosed parking area, while a rustic country retreat offers both inviting shelter and a little whimsy. In a Zurich house (right) where pattern and colour are abundant within, traditional brick contrasts with a bold, patterned door panel.

living

The living area will necessarily be the largest and most flexible part of the house, catering to both public and private activities, offering some amount of comfort and being reflective of personal tastes and style. In a modern, open-plan arrangement, the living space is not separate but is defined by a set of furnishings or partitions. Here in a California house the interior is not only open-plan but a dedicated indoor–outdoor space, where continuous flooring and walls made almost entirely of glass leave few barriers to the surrounding views. Warm colours on the floor, ceiling and built-in units create a sense of intimacy despite the wide open arrangement. Following pages: smart, retro-style furniture and a woven floor-covering form a warm area of living space in another open-plan interior in Singapore (left), while a grander, more formal aspect is given to a high-ceilinged room with monumental glass doors opening to a hard-scaped garden area in Brazil (right).

Smaller living spaces with more colour and variety still have a modern edge. A sumptuous interior for an apartment in Brazil (opposite) features plush furnishings in deep colours along with an array of artworks, while maintaining a modern sense of balance. A more spartan take on living space in the UK (above, left) benefits from natural wood-plank floors, vivid modern sofas, abundant natural light and a focus on the outside view. A taste for retro furnishings can be accommodated with a more inward focus (above, right). Here, a preference for comfort and rich colour is carefully indulged within an elegant modern framework.

cooking & eating

Kitchens and bathrooms are largely functional spaces that sometimes struggle to keep to a modern style. But kitchen space has increased in the last century and so has our taste for up-to-date fittings and appliances. The eat-in kitchen must perform another function, whether it is just a family table or it doubles as an official dining space. To keep the multi-functioning area from appearing too multi-focused, materials can be kept to a minimum in both cooking and eating areas, and furnishings can be pared down to help the flow in and around the cooks' domain.

An elegant, wood-lined cooking and dining area (above) has the appearance and feel of a formal dining space, as the kitchen is in the raised area at right. Opposite, top: a modern kitchen/bar in the UK (right) is scarcely more up-to-date than the kitchen/eating area of a stylishly renovated French chateau (left). Opposite, bottom: efficient island kitchens in Australia and Long Island contrast with slightly more rustic elegance in an old stone house in a small French village.

Pared-down Modernism and high-gloss finishes (below, left) keep the kitchen and eating area calm and uncluttered but still brilliantly colourful and appealing. Uncluttered is also still possible with well-loved vintage furniture and weathered floor tiles in the kitchen of a French country house (below, right). The sideboard's robust, utilitarian character is an artful addition to the space. Combining airy formality with efficient use of space and a focus on the beautiful lustre of hardwood, this house on the protected woodland coast of northeast Australia (opposite) revels in the natural elements while also keeping order. Natural light, always an advantage in a kitchen, floods this space through large glass walls and clerestory windows. Following pages: more cooking and eating with natural light in a mid-century California house with preserved period units and partition (left), and the more traditional window openings of a smaller but cosily efficient kitchen space in San Francisco (right).

Modern efficiency combines with cool elegance in a studied contrast of materials and styles. This kitchen block (opposite) presents a shift of colour and contrasts with more delicate elements, such as the crystal chandelier and ornamental tap, in the living/kitchen area of a colour-filled Sydney residence. A California hillside house (above) equipped with industrial-style rolling metal shutters and a definitive indoor–outdoor character has an equally robust approach to the kitchen furniture. The freestanding unit offers both a sense of flexibility and hardy utility. It also acts as a partition that defines the cooking area from the living space beyond. The open walls mean that ventilation is rarely a problem.

entertaining

There are those who would say that the days of the formal dining room are over. But then there are those who would disagree. Even as part of an open-plan interior, a dining space still holds dramatic appeal. Whether for large dinner parties or more casual gatherings, the existence of a defined space for sitting and eating with friends or invited guests creates a feeling of warmth and the potential for sparkling conversation or debate. Designer Karim Rashid's holiday home (below, left) is as colourful as his own oeuvre. The room is full of bold tones, from the pink gloss of the mid-century style chairs to the vivid wall colour, but even with the dynamic diptych on the wall, the space is well composed. A far more neutral atmosphere prevails in the dining area of this modern design in Singapore (below, right), where the focus is on natural wood and the view through large planes of glass. A clean-lined, double-height residence (opposite) combines formality and delight, as eclectic furnishings and a striking wall mural create a distinctive dining space. Following pages: a more studied formality reigns in a UK apartment (left) and a New York loft apartment (right).

working

The home office has come a long way from the artist's studios and gentlemen's libraries of old. Today's home work spaces combine personal taste with sometimes only bare functional necessities, as in this office in a renovated Chilean farmhouse (opposite, left). Here, minimal office furnishings are an elegant design gesture, allowing the natural materials and vernacular features of the house to take precedence. They emphasize the fact that the house is primarily a place of retreat. A more traditional desk heaped with books and artifacts sits in an early 20th-century California house (opposite, right). A simple white space with a handy window for gazing off in thought leaves room for creativity in a Danish house (above, left), and a colourful corner demonstrates a playful attitude towards working at home in Karim Rashid's holiday retreat (above, right).

sleeping

The bedroom is a pocket of luxury and private taste, which is especially effective in a modern, open-plan house. Whether the room itself is an attic retreat or only separated by a partition, the bedroom is a chance to revel in material and aesthetic comfort. A bedroom in the eaves of a renovated farmhouse (below, left) keeps to a simple palette that emphasizes the character of the silvery aged ceiling beams and plank wood flooring. With its wood-burning stove, wood-panelled walls, fleece rug and plush counterpane, this bedroom in a forest cottage (below, right) is the epitome of cosy without being overstuffed. The bare elegance of finely finished wood and natural concrete (opposite) is made more alluring by the flow of natural light and the open bathing/sleeping arrangement of a Brisbane house. As the house is set on a narrow site on a busy street, the rooms were created with the feeling of quiet, light-filled sanctuary.

There is something very luxurious, or, for those of us in cooler climates, slightly exotic, about a sleeping space that opens directly to the outdoors. The sense of luxury in this Brazilian retreat (opposite) is enhanced by the fine-grade wood cladding and polished wood floors. The pattern of the gridded windows mimics the rhythm of the louvred skin, which covers the external walls and the large sliding door that opens onto the poolside deck. Indoors and outdoors, sunlight and shade are layered in an unusual bedroom and courtyard arrangement in an Australian apartment (below, left), while a sleek modern Turkish house features a sleeping/ lounging nook in a converted attic that recalls the casual splendour of an oriental pavilion (below, right).

bathing

A modern approach to bathing is to reduce the functional elements to a minimal design, but to instil subtle extravagance in the type and use of material, the amount of natural light or perhaps the placement of the bathing space in an open configuration with the bedroom. In the bathroom of a California house (below) sunlight enters from both windows on opposite sides, and unframed glass eliminates the intrusion of the shower stall, making the whole room open and light. Mirrored panels expand the feeling of space and an open corridor between bedroom and bathroom also makes for a less confining atmosphere in this new London apartment (opposite).

A bathroom need not be overlarge to feel indulgent. Light, surfaces and layout all have an impact on the ambience of any room and are particularly notable in the usually restricted space intended for bathing and showering. Above, from left: a bathroom in the roof space of a Turkish house takes full advantage of space available for a window; natural wood is a key element in this Austrian hillside house, especially here, where it adds a spa-like atmosphere to the bathroom; a large Georgian-style house in suburban Melbourne was renovated and stripped back to bare elements, and the bathroom shows the return to simplicity. In this largely open-plan, Modernist-style house in Los Angeles (left), the bathroom, with its rich, dark tiles and wood panelling, is a distinctly private preserve. A shower stall made of unframed glass that is too beautiful to hide away stands proudly in the bedroom area of an avant-garde New Zealand apartment (opposite).

ambience

It is the general feeling, mood or atmosphere of a room and it is created by a variety of factors. The modern impression has to do with subtle balances of effects that produce a serene, tempered mix, even where there might be striking patterns or colours. Such a balance can be achieved using a palette of neutral and bold, pure white and sharp contrast reaching across the spectrum and the world. Against backgrounds that are plain or patterned, with subtle and stark variations in natural light, texture and contrast, these are rooms inspired by variation and alive to the effects of all of these elements, whether used as a single theme or in rich combinations.

natural light
222

screens
228

fire
230

colour
232

white
238

pattern
244

neutral
246

contrast
252

The Decoration of Houses, published in 1897, was one of the most influential books on interior design in the 19th century. It was written by the soon-to-be-novelist Edith Wharton with her friend, the architect Ogden Codman, Jr. Both were American but had travelled widely through Europe and acquired a taste for restrained, classical interiors. The book, like much of Wharton's fiction, railed against the dark, overstuffed interiors of the Victorian period, and advocated 'the "wise moderation" of the Greeks' and an appreciation for 'simplicity'. In the 20th century, Modernism popularized a taste for pared-down interiors, and an appreciation of singular elements against a plain background. This wasn't quite what Wharton and Codman had in mind, but it was the logical conclusion of that simplifying process.

The modern aesthetic has moved well beyond the novelty of stark white spaces and we have begun to fill rooms with colour, texture and forms that we find pleasing and comfortable. But we are still aware of the appeal of Minimalism, and the ability of a plain background to highlight more ornamental pieces instead of competing with them. However, in the modern house of today it is possible to find a new approach to simplicity, which is more about a judicious choice of features, rather than a bare-bones prescription.

While almost any component of an interior space will affect its visual and sensory impact, there are some particular devices that have more resonance than others. These are things that are fundamental to the overall feeling, or ambience, of a room. Perhaps the most basic influence is the amount of light that a room receives from outside. Artificial lighting is also important, but the effect of natural light on an interior cannot be overstated. A few well-placed windows, a clerestory opening, a skylight and light filtered through shutters or screens all leave different impressions on a room as the sun moves, angles change and brightness fades to twilight. Untempered daylight can be warm or stark, pouring through French windows into a darkened room or magnifying a clean white space.

More subtle, perhaps, are the textures of light and shadow created by screens, whether modern louvred panels in a California house or antique carved sections in a jungle retreat in Bali. Screens

used as partitions create intrigue, only slightly obscuring the view through to other rooms, while screen panels stand as decorative pieces that also help to filter light in soft patterns across a space.

One further influence to do with light and heat is the presence of an open fire in a room. We associate these mostly with the traditional hearth, but the hearth can be a modern block chimney breast that soars into a double-height space, or a hanging oven in painted, moulded steel that offers a colourful spot even when the fire is not in use. Fires also lend a romantic aspect to a bedroom, drawing the focus inward away from other distractions.

The quality of natural light is of course affected by the colour used on walls, floors and furnishings, as is the mood. There might be bold orange accents in a white-themed space or a wall that dominates with a glossy crimson hue. Bright plastic or vinyl furnishings will immediately lift a dining space or sitting area within an open-plan arrangement. Richly toned upholstery helps create an intimacy that relies on the exclusion of natural light for a feeling of retreat. In contrast to bold colour, an all-white palette is still appealing in some situations, whether in a spare, gallery-like space or in a bedroom layered with white-on-white patterns or fabrics.

Along with light and colour, pattern can have a great effect on the visual sense of a room, whether it is used in colours or in neutrals. The most obvious way to introduce pattern may be through wall coverings and soft furnishings, but materials such as wood, metal or concrete might also produce a pattern that adds texture to the room.

And then there are the neutral colours that create a calm, sophisticated atmosphere. We generally think of neutrals as low cream, beige and grey hues, but many colours can be used as a neutral base in the right tone. A neutral palette, like a primarily white one, relies on different materials and textures to create richness in layers and subtle distinctions of colour.

In between and alongside considerations of colour, white or neutral background is the effect of contrast. It can be starkly stated, as in a white-furnished New York loft that is punctuated with pieces of solid black furniture, or more animated using different, brightly coloured elements among a white or neutral ground.

natural light

Natural light is a dynamic feature that continually changes and colours the overall feeling of a room. In temperate regions, the opportunity to use large expanses of glass to light and warm the inside spaces is hard to resist. The effect of these oversized windows is not only to bring natural light to otherwise darkened spaces, but also to open them to the outdoors, to the landscape and the view. Even a small interior can be expanded visually with large windows and generous amounts of light. For a new house south of São Paulo (opposite), the architect created soaring indoor spaces clad in richly coloured tropical wood and glass. The outdoors becomes part of the material and colour scheme as the double-height room almost mimics the giant trees outside. The kitchen area, with a lower height and less window space, remains more secluded. Walls of windows (above, left) create corridors of sunlight through a hallway and kitchen in a Modernist-inspired California home. In the same house, the architects have taken the low horizontal profile of Modernist design a step further by having a sunken kitchen space overlook the courtyard swimming pool (above, right).

A bathroom aglow with natural light seems like grand luxury only achievable in a thoroughly isolated situation. Here in a suburban apartment overlooking Sydney Harbour (below), a wooden screen lets light through, casting soft shadows across the room. It can be lowered to provide more privacy when necessary. Hard materials take on a warmer, softer quality with natural light in a dramatic entrance hall to a house in Singapore (right). Concrete, limestone, marble and the still water of an interior reflecting pool are crossed with light and shadow through narrow vertical strip windows.

ambience natural light

Variations of light and shadow are innumerable and can be tuned to every desired mood or room style. Where more subtle effects are preferable, smaller window openings and opaque filters control the amount of light coming through and ensure privacy. Frosted glass softens daylight entering a warm, wood-lined spa area (opposite, left) that feels surprisingly open in the basement of a London house. Dark slate tiles create a warm rich background with a discreetly placed narrow window in a San Diego house (opposite, right). The reduced aperture allows for a pocket of light that reveals the subtle patterns and texture of the material but is not so harsh as to make it appear washed out. In a spare, all-white space (above, left), a large amount of natural light is both expansive and calming, suited to this meditation room in Venice, California. Light filtered through glass blocks (above, right) creates a luxurious glow on glossy dark surfaces in a modern apartment in São Paulo, Brazil. This allows for the reflection on the mirrored wall to be softer and not overly harsh or glaring.

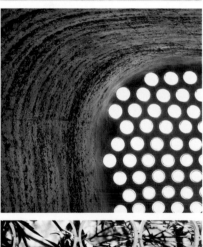

screens

If natural light is like colour in space, then screens are the way to adjust its tone and pattern. In a house where natural light flows freely, screens contribute not only a way of creating privacy but also decorative patterning and texture. In open-plan arrangements screens help to define areas and obscure the view throughout the house without blocking it completely. In tropical climates screens are commonly made of wood carved in intricate designs. They can also be made from antique panels. More modern houses might use louvred panels on the windows or between rooms. Metal mesh, traditional Japanese rice paper and even man-made materials are employed to temper lighting and change the overall tone and style of an interior. Examples from Australia, California, Austria and Britain (opposite) demonstrate the range of possibilities. The iconic Hollywood house (below, left) designed by Lloyd Wright in 1926 features interior screens with a near Eastern influence. A modern house in California (below, right) translates the long horizontal planes to a louvred screen that helps separate the kitchen/dining area.

fire

The modern interior has rediscovered fire as a source of heat and a centre for social gatherings. It is also an object of style. The suspended model (opposite and below, left), first popular in the late 1960s, has been improved with better heat-insulating materials, while the wood-burning stove enjoys a revival in its old-fashioned form (below, right). As we rethink heating in the age of energy awareness, the central heat source not only has romantic appeal but a logical place in our living spaces (right).

colour

It is sometimes said that Minimalism gave us all a fear of colour. However, it was the overuse of colour and profusions of pattern that the spare interior was meant to correct. Many Modernists employed choice blocks of, usually, primary colours to focus attention rather than let the eye be distracted by a host of clamouring tones. Nowadays we have a renewed appreciation for the possibilities of colour, especially in its ability to highlight contrasting or sculptural forms. Glossy surfaces and bold hues (below) contrast with the walls of unpolished concrete. Opposite, clockwise from top left: in a house near Copenhagen simple furnishings are set against muted colours for a subtle effect; in a seaside house on Long Island a white-painted geometric patterned headboard creates a sculptural framework for a deep green wall; an Eames side chair holds a dialogue in shades of blue with a turquoise door; never one to fear the boldest tones, Karim Rashid uses white walls to provide a restful framework for patches of bright tones; Eero Saarinen's classic Tulip chairs and table in clean white are set in the warm olive green dining enclosure of a Zurich house; red becomes a neutral backdrop for black-themed furnishings in a Brazilian apartment. Following pages: deep colours on walls or striking shades on detail surfaces, such as doors and woodwork, are highlighted by contrasting backgrounds or neutral tones; the distinctive shapes of furnishings and features, such as stair-rails, become more prominently sculptural in bold colours; and artist Tomie Ohtake makes concrete a medium for colour with a side table/partition in the dining area of her Brazilian home.

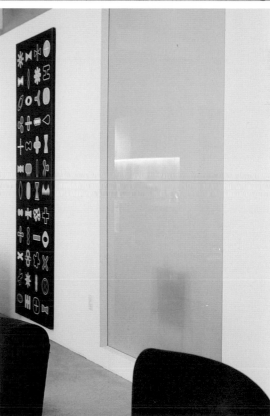

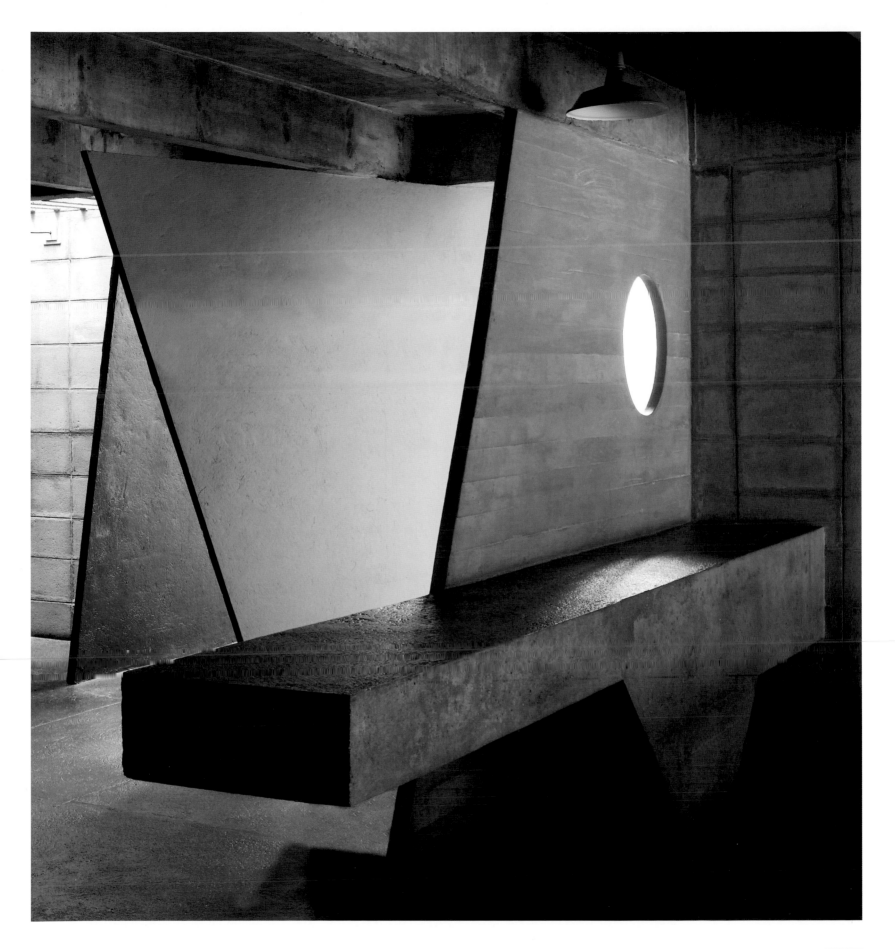

white

White is not just for self-proclaimed purists. Far from being stark or bland, it can be a calming colour, especially in areas where many architectural features are competing and where natural light is prevalent. It may have become a cliché to say that a white background allows other elements to stand out, but the idea still holds true, as does the fact that small spaces feel larger when they're painted white. But white does not necessarily mean a total lack of colour, as it can be enriched with tones varying from cool greys and greens to warmer creams and hints of yellow. Opposite, clockwise from top left: a townhouse in Copenhagen uses white on the floorboards and ceiling to open up a small attic bedroom; clean lines and a glossy surface make a fully modern white space; a New York apartment varies its white palette with soft fabrics and experimental furnishings, such as this Joe Colombo 'sella' chair from 1967; white makes a clean contrast with rugged wood floors in Brazil, and expands a another small bedroom space in France; rooms within the roof space above the Vipp showroom in Copenhagen feel more expansive painted white. A modern house in Bondi, Sydney (below) uses white to magnify natural light and create a cool open-plan interior, with a polished concrete floor adding a warm tone to the white walls and ceiling.

ambience white

Previous pages: gloss and matte finishes distinguish different surfaces and textures in a white-on-white apartment in Manhattan (left); a kind of relaxed, layered effect is created when white is used in combination with other neutral colours, especially when there is enough natural light to bring out the subtle differences in tone,

as in another New York residence (right). These pages: white-washed floorboards, white-painted walls and white kitchen units (opposite, left) contribute variations of material and shade to a white-themed kitchen area of a Danish house. An etched abstract floral pattern on the surface of the units adds subtle patterning to the room.

Marble and concrete can be cool, rather than cold (opposite, right), with daylight streaming through and highlighting golden tones in fashion designer John Rocha's Cap Ferrat retreat in France. A single-level house on Cap d'Antibes, France (above), is given a modern treatment with simple white interiors in an assortment of materials and tones.

pattern

While it is usually true that a little bit of pattern can go a long way in a modern house, particularly when the rest of the spaces are more subdued, it is also true that the ways of displaying pattern are still wide-ranging. But designs need not be fussy or old-fashioned (opposite). Patterned wall-coverings with a modern edge are crisp and expressive in sophisticated tones. An Australian interior (left) embraces vivid patterns without fear, but throughout the house, as here, more lively bursts of pattern are tempered by sections of neutral solids. Modern patterns and strong colours prevail in a French house in Cannes (below, left), where shape is also bold and dynamic, while striking duotone stripes and a bright solid sofa are balanced by the more subdued pattern found in the brick flooring in a room looking out to the garden of a California house (below, right).

neutral

Greys, beiges and other soft tones make a serene, complementary background for more diverse materials and colours, whether in a slick contemporary apartment or a tropical retreat. Natural light is helpful but not essential to a neutral scheme, as the colours can remain subdued whether set in low atmospheric light or spotlit corners. In a New York apartment (left) sleek white floors and furnishings are softened with some neutral hues that come from a range of unlikely materials, including polished concrete, stainless steel, metal mesh and wood. A lower-ground-floor space using unfinished concrete on the walls and stair in the house of a São Paulo art dealer (opposite) becomes a welcoming neutral backdrop for his many large and colourful works of art. The natural irregularities of the concrete in this form give it more texture, interest and warmth. White furnishings also keep the focus on the collection of world-class pieces.

A neutral background suits a modern house as well as older buildings. This neutral palette (opposite) created with various materials and objects becomes a display piece in a toplit hallway. The character and integrity of warm natural wood and old unfinished beams (above) are the focus of an attic bedroom in a renovated French house in a village that retains most of its original structure. Following pages: a classic arrangement in a high-proportioned Paris apartment with large French doors opening to a stone balcony admitting warm, atmospheric natural light to a simply adorned interior (left); a seaside holiday residence in Long Island keeps to a soft, versatile setting for comfortable furnishings and art objects (right).

contrast

Contrast brings visual excitement to a room. Juxtaposing different patterns and colours makes people notice the logic of the space and the objects in it, and how they work with or against one another. Blocks of colour used with a white or black background speak of a bold modern sensibility and cause the furnishings or objects to stand out, so they should be worth looking at. In the light-filled sitting room of a turn-of-the-century house in Cannes, France (left), the designer has used contrast in different ways to make an otherwise simple arrangement more dynamic and vibrant, while still feeling controlled and elegant. Pattern is set against solid colour; a highly polished dark floor and blackened chairs play against the bright yellow block sofa and chairs. These soft shapes sit opposed to the linearity of the chairs at the side, while the strict geometry of the room holds everything in balance. The clean lines highlight the preserved period details of the room, such as the ornamental cornice.

A classic case of contrast is the black-and-white scheme, but even this arrangement has many variations. In a British house in Kensington, London (opposite), Classical-style columns in white seem to float above a dark polished wood floor, and white walls leave the artworks to make their own statements. In a house in Sydney, Australia, where traditional elements are used alongside more contemporary designs (above, left), a retro-looking chequerboard floor and pedestal basin are refreshed by an abstract patterned wall-covering and frameless glass shower enclosure. Black and white make a clean-lined kitchen space even sharper (above, right), while the floor pattern and wood-topped table unit break up the strict colour scheme. Following pages, left: contrast appears in colour and texture in a Brazilian house (top and bottom right) and an apartment full of natural light and rich colours (bottom left). Following pages, right: subtle contrast in a modern Australian interior.

elements

Architectural and decorative details are some of the things that are integral to a house and some that are chosen. They help to create the overall effect of an interior. Objects, soft furnishings and fittings add colour and character. Smaller structural elements, such as stairs, storage units and windows, help define and shape the interior spaces. In some places these will all be of a similar style or material; in others, a well-chosen assortment will convey a dynamic, multifaceted aesthetic. The most successful modern arrangements harmonize an array of elements using balance and proportion as abiding principles.

stairs
264

objets d'art
268

soft furnishings
272

windows
276

display
280

storage
286

lighting
288

fixtures
290

Rooms are compositions made up of architectural features and the pieces that furnish and decorate them. In some houses, whether it is a rustic log cabin, a Modernist glass building or a French chateau, the architecture will affect the style of interior, at least to some degree. Even if the period or style of building itself is not intrusive or immediately obvious, prominent stairs, windows and room openings will have their own effect on the mood and fashion of a space. In addition, they will determine how much natural light enters a room, and how open or secluded the space looks and feels. Although the interiors presented in this section are all rich compilations of such elements, it is worth homing in on specific features to see how these separate influences work within the greater picture.

When they are not hidden away, stairs can bring a wonderfully sculptural presence to a room. In the past a stair might have been considered an intrusion on a space, a structural necessity that blocked circulation and light. However, modern cantilevered, or 'floating' stairs, where there is no supporting under-structure, and sometimes only a minimal rail, let the light flow through the treads horizontally and also downward, perhaps from a top-lit hall. Even as a solid structure, a staircase can take a much more inventive form than we might normally imagine: circular or angled, in robust metal, richly grained wood or glass.

Less functional and more of a luxury item, soft furnishings can be used to add layers of texture and colour to a room, especially when other elements are more subdued. In the best interiors, these fabrics and textiles are used in careful coordination with decorative objets d'art and other furnishings to give contrast in pattern or colour to a more neutral background. Textiles such as rugs, throws, upholstery or curtain fabric can also be used as part of a vibrant composition that is nevertheless controlled and sophisticated.

Windows are another necessary element that can be configured in almost limitless variations of shape, size and position. Clerestory and high-set

windows bring light down into a room without sacrificing privacy. Larger window openings let the outdoor landscaping and light become part of the interior scheme. But windows are not only about letting in as much light as possible. Narrow vertical strips, round window openings or those used in a rhythmic pattern across a wall present controlled bands of light to make an interior more intimate and captivating. Light that enters a room through narrow strips or screened openings has a gentler, more calming presence than the bright fields of sunlight that flood a room with glass walls.

Another architectural element to consider is storage that is built into walls or used as a partition. Like stairs, storage space is sometimes seen as a necessary evil, but in the hands of a more creative individual becomes a virtue. Storage is both a structural and a decorative element, either being completely hidden, say beneath a series of clean white cupboards, or made to stand out as a visual feature, showing off a clever array of shelves with the contents neatly sorted.

The artificial lighting in many of the rooms shown here is provided by fixtures that are themselves objets d'art. Sculptural standing lamps, industrial spotlights or delicate period chandeliers all perform the function of lighting the space while fitting in with the style of the interior. The amount and degree of lighting will always need to be tuned to the space, natural light and time of day, but the style, shape, colour and size of lighting fixtures are as much a part of an overall scheme as the other furnishings and fittings.

Even the most functional fittings confer a design effect on an arrangement, particularly, of course, in bathrooms and kitchens. Taps, sinks, baths and other utilitarian accessories carry themes of modern or heritage, high-tech or classic design. They are complemented by the hard materials in service areas, such as tile, marble or glass, and their polished surfaces reflect other mirrored sections above a sink or bath or kitchen area, giving them even more prominence.

stairs

Stepping up the options. Opposite, clockwise from top left: a wood veneered stair in Sydney, Australia; a narrow walled stair gains character from a playful circular window in a Brazilian townhouse; open wood stairs in a house near Los Angeles; white-washed stucco and narrow strips of local wood keep a stair clean and light in a Sri Lankan retreat. This page, clockwise from top: a Brazilian house in formed concrete, an open-plan Danish apartment and a rammed-earth house in Austria. Following pages: stairs become objects of sculptural intrigue with contrasting colours and materials.

objets d'art

Art is a subjective matter, even more so than a decorative scheme. While elements can always be chosen to fit a certain style, individual objects have to be pleasing for other reasons in addition to period, colour, pattern or texture. And avid collectors will never be deterred by a compromised colour scheme. The trick is in the presentation and choice of items to display in any one arrangement. The colours of a painting are picked up by decorative dishes and candlesticks (above, left); a Japanese-themed room with modern painting and red lacquer in an Australian house (above, right); a pairing of antique Asian wood stools and multimedia abstract art is a serene contrast to the plain interior of this Brazilian house (opposite). Following pages: collections of glassware, jars and finger bowls make pleasing assemblages in small ordered groupings – even a little kitsch is not out of place in a room filled with vivid colours and patterns (left); the most minimal design can become a calm backdrop for a distinctive piece of art (right).

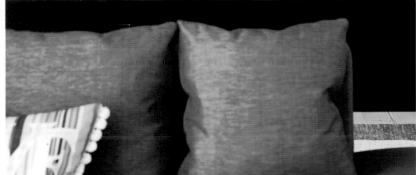

soft furnishings

Fabrics, textiles and upholstery soften hard surfaces and keep colour and texture alive. Opposite, clockwise from top left: a house in Sagaponack, Long Island, highlights the theme of beach and sky with a photographic wall-covering, while the ticking stripe on the bedding recalls the local nautical heritage; vivid patterns and colour brighten a bedroom in an otherwise white-themed palette in designer John Rocha's French seaside house; another seaside house in Montauk, Long Island, maintains its summery feel in pale blue and white; the deep hues used on bedding and walls reflect the style of a Paris pied-à-terre. Simple built-in bench sofas (above, left) get a boost of character with plush upholstery and printed pillows. A modern floral-patterned wall-hanging (above, right) is balanced with solid colours and plainer furnishings. Following pages: sofas in bright patterns make a soft, colourful grouping in a modern house of simple cubic wood volumes (left); a plain room of grand proportions features a plush reading corner with a window seat framed by luxurious draperies and a modern disc lamp (right).

windows

Windows are not just for seeing out of, or for bringing light in. Of course they are necessary for both. But they also make a room seem bigger or smaller, open or intimate. And design patterns carry through to window shape, size and position. A modern house in Dubai (opposite) uses a large, sheltered window to create a cool, light interior, protecting the glass from direct sunlight, while smaller corner windows set above bring in light but also minimize heat gain. A room that is cantilevered out from the hillside into the forest greenery (above) takes advantage of its setting with uncovered windows on three sides, which gives a sense of hovering amid the trees. Following pages: an arched clerestory in Denmark, a vaulted opening in a renovated French chateau, a dramatic grid of windows in Australia and a double-height space with cut-out corner windows with painted surrounds that make an abstract reference to more traditional window frames (left); a seamless corner window surrounding a bath is exposed to light and vegetation (right). The thick trees provide a natural privacy screen.

display

Displaying objects well is an art in itself. Open, floating shelves make objects and books more apparent, particularly against a solid background. In a house north of San Francisco with a retro interior theme (opposite) new shelving is set against old wood panelling and staggered to create a more interesting visual impact. A sleek New York apartment (above) reverses a traditional play of contrast, setting slim white shelves onto a near-black background. The thin profile of the shelves contributes to the 'floating' effect.

More fun with shelving. Previous pages: bold, playful objects are given distinctive display spaces in curving metal shelving (left) and moulded plastic compartments (right). The stacked yellow hexagons in this Los Angeles house can be left open or closed for storage. These pages: walls of books always add life and dimension to a room, even in simple, minimal spaces. A built-in display/cupboard unit curves around the room (above, left), providing maximum storage using a minimum of floor space. In Donna Karan's New York apartment (above, right), walls and shelving in the same dark hue keep the focus on the books, which become a wall of colour, and on the unusual decorative objects. A book-lined home office (opposite) has vertical library shelves and furnishings that recall a previous era, and an oversized window wall that is distinctly contemporary.

storage

Storage is not always about hiding things away. Open shelving and freestanding units can celebrate the artifacts of domestic life and stand as a tribute to small functional objects, while more minimal interiors require deft solutions to the problem of clutter (above). An innovative new house in southwest France (opposite) takes a similar approach to storage, keeping a neat surface with flush veneer cabinets.

lighting

There is much more to a lamp than a mere hanging bulb, which can cast a gloomy atmosphere over the most carefully designed interior. Sculptural or standard, manifold or minuscule, lighting fixtures take their place as design objects by simple virtue of creating light and by inventive ways of surrounding and filtering it. From the boldly futuristic to the supremely delicate, the arrangement of lighting can be the single determining factor in the overall character of a room. Opposite, clockwise from top left: an industrial-style fixture lends an experimental edge to a beachside house in Sydney; a modern layered Magnolia pendant by Autoban contrasts with a traditional plaster ceiling rose in a Turkish apartment; a classic 1960s design is part of a period interior in Palm Beach, Australia; a delicate sculptural nest of twigs recalls the natural twists of driftwood in a Long Island beach house; a retro-style spray of blown glass in an opulent modern Brazilian apartment. An illuminated assemblage by Yuichi Higashionna (right) lights up a New York apartment.

fixtures

Bath tubs, basins, sinks and taps are the hardware that must combine form with function. The humble bath tub has had a radical redesign in this French villa (right), which features a cutting-edge contemporary interior. The moulded composite fitting curves to form a basin at one end and bath at the bottom, making one seamless piece. Glass end pieces emphasize the form and transparency of the water itself. The shelf and mirror above have been shaped to echo the bath and basin construction. Following pages: a freestanding bath has been given a very modern treatment. No longer the claw and ball-footed tubs of the Victorians, smoother and simpler designs prevail even in the most luxurious bathrooms. Clockwise from left: a bathing space that can be opened to the elements and light has an organically shaped contemporary tub; a sharp wooden box-shaped bath with a hillside view in California; another Australian design features a rustic construction in wood plank; a platform bath makes a grand statement and provides room for services underneath; a pure-form, high-sided tub is all about indulgence.

Style on tap: the functional objects that finish off a well-designed bathing space. A New York loft apartment with a sophisticated modern interior (above, left) has a new take on the farmhouse kitchen sink, as a double-basin solution in an en-suite bathroom. Blocks of blue resin (above, right) make a colourful splash against white marble and dark wood in a California house. Stainless steel is still the favoured option for fixtures (left), whether used with stone, marble or, as in a house in Provence, against a dark-coloured wall. The combination of stainless-steel fittings and a mirrored wall panel have an enduring, clean-lined appeal. A modern minimal bathroom space in a Danish apartment (opposite) keeps everything refreshingly simple.

furniture

Luxury or necessity, function or form. The choice of furniture for the modern house does not depend on specific trends or adherence to rules of purity, but rather is based in guiding principles of simplicity, functionality and beauty. From iconic Modernist-period favourites to latter-day interpretations, works of experimental design and more comfortable alternatives, the modern house can accommodate a surprisingly wide range of styles and periods. Even beloved antique or vintage pieces can work in an uncluttered modern space as long as an overall harmony prevails.

sculptural
302

built in
306

retro
310

multi-functional
312

vintage
314

simple
318

plush
322

iconic
324

If rooms are personal expressions, then individual items of furniture are surely even more so. Nobody wants a room in a colour they do not enjoy or a chair they find distasteful. But the modern house welcomes many styles because, overall, the interior will suggest a sense of harmony between elements, architecture, surfaces and light: all the things that create the general atmosphere. Into that backdrop, a genuine Louis XVI armchair can feel just as suitable as a Philippe Starck 'Ghost' version. If the following pages tell us anything about a stunning modern interior it is that versatility rather than any conformity to style is the rule.

As furniture and sculpture crossed paths in the 20th century, some protested that comfort was being sacrificed for form. But there will always be an aesthetic appeal in pure forms, whether or not they accommodate the human body as 'extensions of our limbs', as Le Corbusier would have it. The chair as a sphere or as sliced conical shape, the table as constellation of discs; these are works that provoke thoughtful scrutiny, and are seldom overlooked.

Even compared to the avant-garde in furnishings, nothing says modern and bespoke so much as built-in furniture. Practitioners of the Arts and Crafts movement used built-in bookcases and seating to integrate themes and patterns throughout their interiors. A house by Charles Rennie Mackintosh or Frank Lloyd Wright, to name but two, would not be complete without the many cabinets and other highly specified functional amenities built into the design. For the Farnsworth House in Illinois, Mies van der Rohe created a large piece of built-in cabinetry that is both storage and necessity: a central core that contains two bathrooms, a kitchen unit and all the cupboards. Today's built-in furnishings are perhaps less imposing, but still add to the streamlined efficiency of the interior, leaving space for movement and for other objects to enjoy more prominence.

Like Mies' wooden core at the centre of the Farnsworth House, and like the furnishings of medieval European houses, pieces that perform more than one function are often essential in the modern, open-plan house. They make the best use of space and have a very satisfying dual purpose. A sofa that includes a side table or one that also forms a bookcase are ingenious design solutions that most people find irresistible and make a house feel custom-made for the occupants.

While design icons and custom-made built-ins are well suited to the modern interior, it would be disingenuous to believe that we could banish older or even antiquated pieces. If anything, the space and light of a modern house will allow the character of a vintage piece or collection to shine. In the following pages there are renovated farmhouses with modern furnishings and fittings and newly built houses enlivened with older chairs, tables and cabinets. There are examples of retro furnishings, including postwar upholstered armchairs with lovingly aged wood frames and vibrant futuristic forms from the 1960s and 1970s. Sometimes it is the very contrast that makes the house feel personal and up-to-date.

For those who do not wish to confine their furnishing choices to pieces by the Modernist masters but who still have an admiration for the simplicity and utility of those forms, there are new designs that carry on the key concepts. Sofas and chairs that maintain the low horizontal profile appear in more varied hues than the originals and in modified forms that play on the Modernist obsession with geometry. Such pieces acknowledge the influence of earlier designs but boast a contemporary edge, and newfound appeal.

But modern interiors do not have to be dominated by such classic forms and their descendants. There is always room for luxurious upholstered furnishings. Deep sofas in rich velvet fabrics make a room feel like an indulgence even if it is lined in polished concrete floors and white walls. An ornate chair, table or chest becomes an object of interest, as much a work of art as something more sculptural in the uncluttered modern setting.

However, the icons of Modernist furniture design are still some of the best-loved pieces of all time, must-have objects for design enthusiasts and architecture devotees. They are easy to spot and as impressive now as they ever were in their combinations of function and form: Mies van der Rohe's Barcelona chair, first created for the German pavilion at the 1929 Barcelona exposition, the Wassily chair by Marcel Breuer, the Eames lounge chair and footstool of 1956, Le Corbusier's cubic Petit Confort and Grand Confort, Josef Hoffmann's Kubus and Florence Knoll's equally rectilinear two-seater. Some examples of these designs grace the new modern interiors in the pages that follow, demonstrating quite clearly the timeless appeal of the building blocks of the modern aesthetic.

sculptural

Furniture is always something more than functional. The clean modern interior is the ideal backdrop for pieces that approach the form and effect of sculpture. But unique or high-concept sofas, chairs and tables do not always need stand-alone status; in fact, their functionality is often what makes them most engaging. A boldly shaped, vivid red upholstered chair (opposite, left) stands out handsomely against the classic modern backdrop of this mid-century residence in Silverlake, California, designed by Richard Neutra. Modern zig-zag acrylic bar stools (opposite, right) complement the stainless-steel catering table on the polished granite floor of a contemporary New Zealand residence. A ball-shaped chair made from stiffened rope (above, left) carries a nautical theme in this cottage in Victoria, Australia, while a London house (above, right) contrasts dark tropical wood with avant-garde furnishings throughout. Here a 'Blo-Void 2' chair in polished and anodized aluminium with aluminium mesh designed by Ron Arad sits like a work of art.

A 'pappardelle' chair in woven brass mesh by Ron Arad (left) resembles a softly unfurled ribbon. Below, from left: a moulded fibreglass 'felt' chair by Marc Newson contrasts with the 1950s decor of this Los Angeles house; a bentwood seat shows the mid-century taste for wood-grained veneer; the upholstered 'bella' chair by Twentieth keeps to the mid-century theme in a John Lautner-designed house in Los Angeles. Opposite, clockwise from top left: a vivid ovoid chair and ottoman make a pleasant reading corner next to an oversized window; a scrolling cardboard 'wiggle' chair by Frank Gehry; an adapted wing chair design forms a cosy headboard enclosure in a modern Turkish residence; a set of 1965 'luar' chairs by Ross Littell create a modern stir in an Italian townhouse; a moulded plastic chair brightens a cool Modernist corner in a key-side home in Florida.

built in

One of the marvels of modern design was the freeing up of interior space by making furniture and storage a part of the internal structure of a house or apartment. This solution provides not only a clutter-free environment, but also a seamless interior and the most efficient use of space, since built-in units become part of a wall or partition and storage can take advantage of every void. A contemporary California house designed in the Modernist spirit (opposite) features a built-in breakfast table and storage that is set perfectly within the lower-level space. This leaves the wall free to be fitted with windows reaching over 3m (10ft) in height. A London residence (above, left) has an oriental flavour with specially chosen reclaimed teak used throughout, including on this partition and bench unit. Another British apartment with a similar partition and bench combination (above, right) has cupboards subtly incorporated into the high-gloss unit.

Although built-in furniture is often associated with **Arts and Crafts** or **Modernist** designs, it is essential in any streamlined minimal scheme. Built-in pods for lounging or sleeping (above) add to the futuristic feel of this New York apartment. The padded niches have the compact efficiency of spacecraft seating or boat design. A more traditional take on built-in furniture in this modern California house (opposite): the few additional objects and furnishings make a minimalist statement, while the dark wood, rugs and upholstery create a warm atmosphere.

retro

Almost anything from any previous decade could be called retro, but here we are considering furnishings that have the shape and style of designs from the 1940s to the 1970s: not old enough to be considered antique, and not belonging to the pantheon of architect-designed pieces of the Modernist oeuvre. Retro implies softly curved edges, a quality of materials and of course an air of nostalgia. Rounded corners with vaguely aerodynamic styling and newly popular space-age patterning combine to recall a feeling of postwar optimism and design flair. A 1960s California Modernist house (left) keeps its period charm with rattan-wrapped club chairs and retro-print cushions. Opposite, clockwise from top left: a Scandinavian chair makes a perfect place for reading in a modern-style Los Angeles house; a Brazilian house features a Filo armchair by Francisco Fanucci with a cowhide pattern reminiscent of the 1950s; another Brazilian house showcases a 'ball' chair – designed by Eero Aarnio in 1966, it has become an symbol of the era; a small side table in a modern Singaporean apartment has the curves and wood veneer surface of early modern pieces.

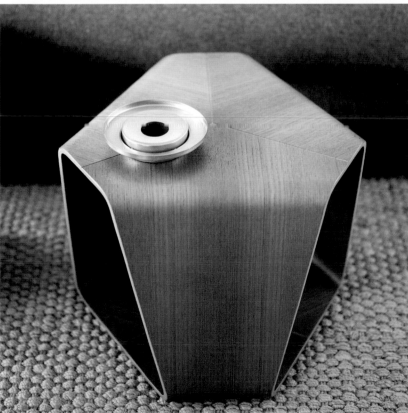

multi-functional

A lot of built-in furniture is designed to perform more than one task; for example, a bookcase can be made to act as a partition or bed frame. But many modern moveable furnishings, from the early decades of the 20th century to current designs, incorporate more than one function into a single piece. Fashion designer Donna Karan's warm but minimal black-and-white-themed New York apartment (opposite) features this elegant, black-lacquered sofa-and-side-table combination. Designer Jonny Detiger's New York city eyrie (below, left) displays works of the his own design, such as this stereo-turntable-and-seating unit. The mirrored panels complement the high polish on the floor surface. A Brazilian residence (below, right) is full of lovingly presented retro pieces, such as this early modern sofa-and-bookcase.

vintage

Vintage can mean anything that is not contemporary and is not of a specific style. In the context of the modern house, we use the word to refer to furnishings that were produced before the Second World War but do not come under the 'modern' rubric. Whether antique family heirlooms or just beloved pieces that show the style and perhaps even the wear of age, vintage elements are particularly appealing on their own, when they add period character without overwhelming the overall ambience of the modern interior. Right, clockwise from top left: a cottage in Australia combines deep modern colours with a few choice furnishings from past generations, such as this rustic sideboard; a set of leather travelling cases make a quirky side table in a cool white scheme; in a Paris apartment that fuses period architecture with modern art and design, an aged wood chest of drawers has been recast as a base for a modern basin and fixtures; an Australian fashion designer's country retreat is all modern spaces with some inspiring vintage objects, such as this unusual little chest. A carved wood secretary with ornate detailing (opposite) makes a period contribution to a clean modern British interior.

furniture vintage

Vintage furnishings that recall another time and place provide a romantic touch to an otherwise clean-lined or minimal space. A Paris apartment (opposite) retains some of its period features, such as this built-in cabinet, while elsewhere a more modern approach has been used. A carved wood four-poster bed with intricate patterns (below, left) is set off by a white-washed wall, plain white bedding and smooth wood flooring in a modern Sri Lankan house, while an old ironwork bedstead (below, right) has been given a new lease of life with vivid striped covering on the mattress and cushions, and a prominent place on the hardwood deck overlooking a pond.

simple

When Mies van der Rohe said, 'Less is more,' he was presenting the concept that fewer items can have a larger impact than an overabundance. This, of course, rests on the premise that those few things have some innate quality and integrity that makes them more worthwhile than a collection of other things. Simple furnishings are not those that adhere to the styles of the Minimalists' palette, or the Modernists' even, but those that have a pure basic form and material that makes them satisfying as integral objects and as functional pieces. They may emphasize the Minimalist sensibility, but their delight is the actual look and feel rather than an ideal. Right, clockwise from top: compressed layers of wood form a table and benches for the garden of a French country house; a pair of wood stools have the enduring appeal of pure forms in wood; a Provençal farmhouse features seats made of hollowed wood; the exotic grain and colour of tropical hardwood takes precedence in this Brazilian house, where plain white furnishings provide a mellow contrast. An Austrian hillside house (opposite) with a pervading aesthetic of wood keeps furnishings to the natural theme.

The simple pleasure of pure white is evident throughout fashion designer John Rocha's French holiday home (above). White-covered upholstery and walls are warmed up by wood flooring and modern rattan chairs. A Los Angeles designer's home (opposite) keeps to a pure white palette with a distinctly contemporary feel. The clean horizontals of the sofa, chairs and table mimic the interior architecture, making a thoroughly modern space. Colour is provided by accents and by the greenery visible through large window walls.

plush

'Plush modern' might sound like an oxymoron, but there is no rule against comfort or soft fabrics in a well-designed space. The lilac velvet sofa of this grandly proportioned Paris apartment (opposite) not only helps to soften the room but mediates between period details, such as the classical-style columns and bas-relief over-door panel, and the works of contemporary art and design. The soft furnishings in this California house (above) are colourful and curvy without being garish. They also have a slightly retro style that is a nod to Californian Modernism. The velvet-upholstered pieces vary in shape and hue, from the curving corner sofa, circular stool and tub chair to the square sofa seating. But the low profile of all of the furniture against the plain walls keeps the room calm and allows the large artwork to stand out.

iconic

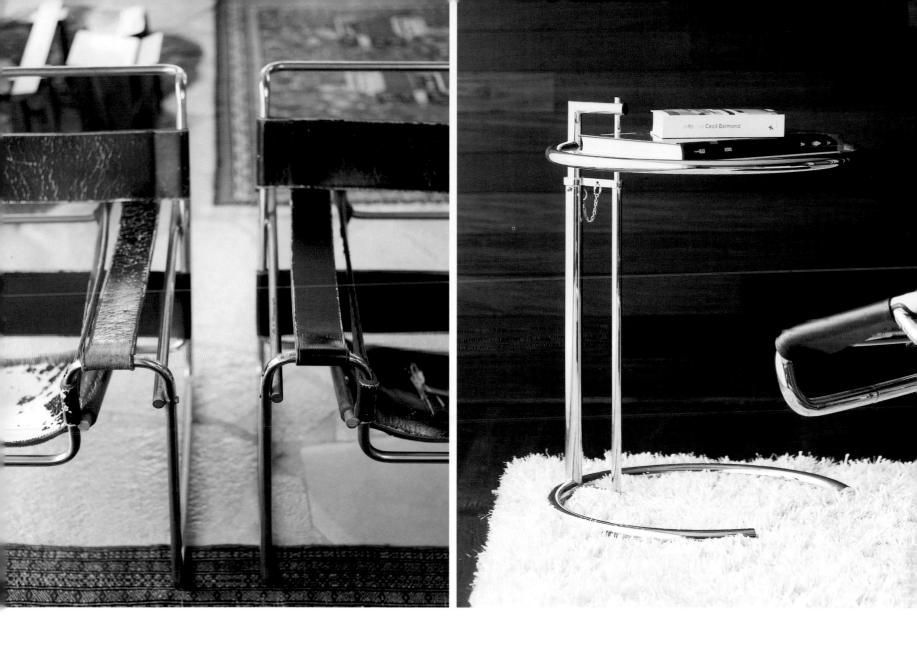

Although the modern house can and does work with almost any kind of furniture, as long as there is balance, there is no question that certain icons will always strike the note of great moments in design. This moulded plywood dining chair by Charles and Ray Eames (opposite, left) has survived many imitations since it was introduced in the mid-1940s. It is still a popular classic. The Diamond chair by Harry Bertoia (opposite, right) was designed in 1952 and produced by Knoll under close supervision of the designer himself.

The Wassily chair designed by Marcel Breuer in 1925 (above, left) was revolutionary in its use of bent tubular steel. It was inspired by bicycle design and was originally created for the rooms of the painter Wassily Kandinsky at the Dessau Bauhaus. This adjustable side table (above, left) was originally created by Eileen Grey as part of the E-1027 house that she helped to design with Jean Badovici in Roquebrune, near Monaco, in the late 1920s. Here it composes part of a Modernist vignette, alongside a Le Corbusier LC4

chaise longue in a bedroom lined in richly coloured hardwood. Following pages: a Connecticut house designed by Mies van der Rohe retains elements of the Farnsworth House and his Barcelona Pavilion. It is fittingly furnished with 'comfort' sofas and armchairs by Le Corbusier in the living area and with cantilevered tubular steel dining chairs designed in the late 1920s by Mies van der Rohe and Lilly Reich, along with a glass-topped dining table in a similar aesthetic.

furniture iconic

outdoors

Sweeping interior spaces that flow freely out of doors are usually considered the purview of warm climates, as are extensive 'outdoor rooms' that encourage living and entertaining to happen outdoors as well as in. But people who are driven more by ingenuity and creativity than by temperature find ways to make external spaces radiant even in cooler climates, as some of the houses here can demonstrate. One need only be reminded of the manicured gardens of a French chateau or Italian villa to see that outdoor living is not a novel concept and not something restricted to tropical climates.

garden design
334

courtyard
338

planting
342

lounging
344

vista
348

terrace
350

al fresco
354

pool
356

It was the Viennese-born architect Rudolf Schindler who, after moving to California in the 1920s to oversee projects for Frank Lloyd Wright, popularized the idea of outdoor rooms. The house/studio space that he designed was originally conceived as a basic 'camper's shelter' and consisted of what he deemed to be 'an entirely new spatial interlocking between the interior and garden'. So taken was he with the temperate climate that he originally designed the bedrooms as no more than sheltered sleeping porches. Schindler's Kings Road house is now considered one of the icons of early modern architecture and his views on opening houses up to their natural environment continue to have an impact on contemporary design.

We can see this influence in the many houses that include living spaces for the outdoors. These are not merely tables and chairs set out in the garden, but genuinely free-flowing space inside and out. Setting does have a significant impact on how open a house can be to the elements. But it does not have to deter would-be sun/sky-seekers from maximizing whatever access they do have to an outdoor space.

One of the greatest effects of an outdoor living space is the way it promotes the flow of people between areas. When the floor is level with or in the same material as the immediate terrace or patio, it encourages people to carry on from one space to another. Wide door openings and, of course, large, sliding glass doors also help the life of the house to spill out and in freely.

Along with ease of access, most of the houses in these pages have an alluring outdoor space. There are few views as inviting as a beautifully laid out garden glimpsed through a window or doorway. As to the style, great modern garden design can draw on the traditional approaches of the Mediterranean villa and the tropical house, the formal gardens of Europe, as well as more current ornamental and artistic schemes. Whichever style holds sway, it confirms a modern idea that good landscape design helps to make the outdoors not only an enjoyable place to be, but also an important, and connected, part of the house.

When Rudolf Schindler began designing low-cost homes, it was his ambition to include terraces, courtyards and roof decks whenever possible, so that even a small house could feel the luxury of space and sky. As well as including a well-designed garden, today's rooms for outdoor living are often

created through built features, such as a wide terrace, an enclosed courtyard or an outdoor swimming pool.

Whether it is a wide wooden deck, a flagstone patio or a gravel seating area, a terrace extends the living space of the house, making even a modestly sized dwelling feel expansive. Similarly, a sheltered courtyard around which the rooms are organized becomes part of the house while also offering a taste of open air. While this kind of arrangement is most often found in tropical or desert climates, architects are incorporating variations of courtyard designs more frequently in houses all around the world to allow natural light to penetrate the mass of the house, create transparency through the volumes and improve passive heat gain.

Swimming pools are a luxury amenity. They are also healthy and great entertainment for adults and children. But their contribution to the house is aesthetic, too. The swimming pool brings the element of water to the hard landscape or green of the garden and creates new opportunities for designing both living space around the poolside and vistas across the water. Terraced arrangements can provide seating and access on different levels, or

a seamless design can make the outdoor swimming pool a part of the interior.

But whether or not a pool is part of your house plan, the planting of the outside space is crucial. It may also influence the indoor atmosphere if glass is used and the plants are employed to create a lush privacy screen. And for people who want to spend a great deal of time moving between outdoors and in, their enjoyment of the whole range of spaces will be greater if there has been some thought about the functional aspect of the garden or terrace. Areas that are configured for cooking and eating or just for lounging and entertaining can be as comfortable as interior rooms. As with the indoors, the success of the outdoor space also depends on lighting, in addition to the landscaping and planting.

A small area should not be a deterrent to outdoor living. A house in the Australian bush or in the jungle of Bali might have more ample grounds to work with, but the New York balcony or the enclosed courtyard deserves even more thought, since the use and the view might be limited. If you do not have generous or year-round access to an outdoor living space, there is even more reason to make the most of a place in the fresh air and sun.

garden design

If the garden is indeed an 'outdoor room' then the layout, pattern and colour might be as well orchestrated as a highly crafted interior. Vividly painted garden walls, oversized sculpture, rustic pots and artistic vessels, fountains, reflecting pools, lamps and pavers: these are just some of the elements that are used in gardens in all kinds of locations to make the outdoor space a wonderfully inviting area for relaxing, entertaining and meditating. Details of garden vignettes from Australia, Italy, France, Bali, the UK and Brazil (opposite) demonstrate how simple arrangements of plants, ornaments and hardscape are used to create striking spaces. Even antiquated elements can be used to create a modern aesthetic. An unusual standing lamp (right) makes a quirky flourish in a garden space in Cannes.

These spaces can accommodate grand gestures as well as detailed arrangements, and traditional houses do not necessarily mean traditional gardening. The modern attitude towards crisp geometry and clean spaces can create the perspectives and intricacies of a sculpture garden while providing habitable spots for sitting, eating, conversing. The garden of a restored chateau in the south of France (above) is articulated by artistic panels and sculptural, cubic furnishings. In a California house (opposite, top left) large pivoting doors line the pool terrace and are set off by palm trees, while in Provence an old stone farmhouse has been updated and brought to life with bold modern garden design that juxtaposes old-growth trees and plants with strict geometric shapes (opposite, right). A new-build Australian house (opposite, bottom left) sits low in the landscape with a curved and terraced lawn that harmonizes with the low horizontal structure.

courtyard

Courtyards are serene and enchanting spaces. They offer fresh air and sunlight as well as the protection of enclosed private rooms. Like a walled garden, they can become spaces for rarefied plants or kitchen herbs. They also provide a centre around which the other rooms can be arranged, to face trees or plants and light. A house in Sri Lanka (opposite, left) is centred around a courtyard where a revered tree holds a hanging seat for a meditative break. In Sydney, the suburban surroundings are undetectable in this peaceful courtyard eating area (opposite, right). Even in more urban surroundings (above, left), the courtyard provides respite from the noise and clutter of the world outside. John Rocha's retreat in France (above, right) contains several spaces where the countryside is gently mitigated by low white walls and simple, well-chosen ornaments.

Islamic architecture has provided some of the best examples in history of the use of water flowing through built spaces. Modern design contributes a fresh approach to bringing pools and channels of water indoors and around living spaces. In Bali, a magical arrangement of a courtyard walkway across a planted reflecting pool is both exotic and welcoming (above). The weathered, mossy stone contrasts with the clean, orderly stone path, and the branches become sculptural against the neat rectangular walls and openings. A new modern house in Singapore (opposite) adheres to the use of sharp rational forms, but the effect is softened by the pool flowing in close proximity to the house and the reflective surface it provides for the strong vertical elements.

planting

For many people gardens and outdoor spaces mean greenery. But the ways trees, hedges, grass and potted plants are used in modern design, or the way the design is used to frame a verdant portrait, make the garden much more than just a spot of green. One possible benefit of our water-consciousness (and perhaps restrictions on water usage) is that the perfect rectangle of lawn is increasingly being replaced by more varied and interesting plantings that make the most of the local climate conditions and also complement the natural setting of the house. Opposite: existing trees are accommodated by wood decking in Brazil, stone pavers in Australia and by the creation of a courtyard pond in Bali. Elsewhere, low-level, low-maintenance planting stands out against linear cladding and highly ordered glass-and-steel walls, a glazed wall has an unobstructed view over low-growing plants, and the courtyard space of a glass-and-steel structure feels fresh and welcoming with prairie-style plantings. A house in California (right) uses lushly planted pathways between glazed spaces to filter light and views between rooms.

lounging

Garden spaces are made for relaxation, especially when the design has been carefully orchestrated to create comfortable areas for lounging while also maximizing the view and greenery. The shelter of an overhanging roof (opposite, left) makes a secluded spot for enjoying the natural vegetation and poolside landscaping in a modern Brazilian house, while the garden of a refurbished chateau in Provence (opposite, right) is a distinctly modern design that overflows with native plants. The forested coastal region of Guarujá, south of São Paulo, is the setting for this striking modern open-plan house with floating deck and swimming pool overlooking the beach (below, left), while a courtyard pool is surrounded by greenery in a suburban California house (below, right). Following pages, left: the gazebo has had a sophisticated modern makeover in Bali, Australia and California. From traditional wood pavilions to extended terraces to tented shelters, imaginative designs take advantage of site and the particular luxury of bringing comfort to the outdoors. Following pages, right: a Los Angeles barn-style house exploits its monumental door to make the poolside garden an extension of the living space; designer Todd Oldham's Pennsylvania holiday home features a pavilion set on a raised platform that can be turned to face or shelter from the sun or wind; more tropical-style lounging in Brazil and the Mediterranean.

vista

Even if a house has a only a small outdoor space, there is still the opportunity for creating a more expansive feeling with a well-orchestrated sightline. A beautiful view of the natural terrain is often left to chance in the garden, but there is something to be said for encouraging the obvious, for orienting a house or garden pavilion or even a modest seating area so that the full effect of a dramatic vista is not only seen but felt as a part of the experience of the house and site. An unencumbered view is not always the most intriguing. Here, in the lush hills of the Sri Lankan landscape (opposite), the eye is drawn to the terrace and the radiating branches that filter the view of the river and jungle beyond, while the excitement of a dramatic view (below) is heightened with an infinity pool that appears to flow out of the house and over a sheer drop.

terrace

The indoor–outdoor nature of modern living could not be possible without the terrace. The physical extension of habitable floor space into the garden, roof or balcony is a signal that the life of the house continues beyond the walls and even further outwards. The terrace is an invitation to step outside, and the arrangement of furnishings or objects there are an incentive to relax and stay a while. In Noosa, Australia (above, left), where protected national forest follows the northeast coastline, a shaded deck with open metal railings becomes a hillside viewing platform. The roof terrace as breakfast nook in a house in the Long Island countryside (above, right) provides a view over forests and farmland, while the deck of a beachside cottage offers the quintessential lounging and meditation space (opposite, left). The Brazilian jungle is the back garden of this modern holiday home (opposite, right), with luxurious planked hardwood decking all around that continues through the house. Following pages: stunning terrace settings with views of a river in Noosa, Queensland, Brazilian jungle, a pond in Todd Oldham's garden and inland waterway Surfers Paradise in Queensland.

al fresco

The Italians may have coined the most familiar term for dining outdoors but the idea has caught on in most parts of the world. Just as Epicurus believed that 'we should look for someone to eat and drink with before looking for something to eat and drink', we are also conscious of where we eat. In the garden we want to enjoy the fresh air, the touch of breeze and the view. In some parts of the world, open-air dining is a way of life; in others, we make the most of sunny mornings, warm afternoons and sultry evenings as they happen. Palm trees and a palisade roof (left) contrast with the bright modernity of the house interior. The outdoor table and benches add a rustic touch. Outdoor dining is done in casual splendour in a California garden (opposite, top right) where a crystal chandelier hangs from an arching tree and high-back upholstered chairs pull up to a rough-hewn table lit with trays of candles. Modern panels form a screen for a corner seating and eating area in a garden in Provence (opposite, top left). Opposite, bottom, from left: outdoor dining in Brazil, the Danish countryside and upstate New York.

pool

No longer just a place to take some healthy exercise, the swimming pool is a setting for peaceful respite and reflective beauty, and contributes a soothing, elegant atmosphere to indoor as well as outdoor spaces. Though modern versions tend to favour rectangular shapes over the curving backyard pools of previous decades, there is still abundant variation in style and design. A bold modern house in Singapore (above) contrasts curving sheets of metal with tropical hardwood and a deck at pool level that gives the structure the appearance of a house boat. A restored mid-century house in Los Angeles boasts a daring elliptical cliffside pool (opposite).

The privacy of the pool area of this 1930s house in Beverly Hills (left) is assured by the thick trees that have been preserved all around the garden. Below, from left: the design for an Australian house uses its hillside setting to spectacular effect, as the water is allowed to spill gently over the edge of the terrace and in the direction of a expansive view; modern pools in Singapore and Provence maintain a clean linear shape. Opposite: rectilinear pool designs combine with lush plantings and cool modern furnishings. Following pages: the drama of architecture combined with water in a modern Brazilian house; and in the misty hills above Santa Barbara, California, and the forested suburbs of Brisbane.

architects & designers

AFGH (Zurich)
www.afgh.ch
60, 80, 166, 187, 233, 270

Agape Design (Mantova, Italy)
www.agapedesign.it
171, 305, 371, 374

Aleks Istanbullu Architects
(Los Angeles)
www.ai-architects.com
13, 79, 81, 91, 96, 152, 186,
309, 342

Eric Allart (Paris)
www.ericallart.fr
52, 270, 316

Amy Finn Bernier Architect
(Los Angeles)
www.amyfinnbernier.com
90, 167, 193, 236

Andrew Lister Architect
(Auckland)
www.andrewlisterarchitect.com
117, 270, 329

Architectus (Sydney)
www.architectus.com.au
125, 149

AREA Designs (Bali)
www.areadesigns.com
40–41, 141, 146, 153, 334, 340,
342, 346, 349

Assembledge+ (Los Angeles)
www.assembledge.com
259, 294

Autoban (Istanbul)
www.autoban212.com
165, 288, 305

Baker Kavanagh Architects
(Sydney)
www.bka.com.au
90

Ban Shubber Associates
(London)
www.banshubber.com
6, 54, 173, 236

Bark Design Architects
(Noosa Heads, Australia)
www.barkdesign.com.au
23, 103, 197, 350

Barton Myers Associates, Inc.
(Norfolk, USA)
www.bartonmyers.com
9, 28, 117, 201, 214, 218, 329,
343, 344, 362

**Bauart Architekten und Planer
AG** (Zurich)
www.bauart.ch
27, 117, 238

Florence Baudoux (Paris)
luma@noos.fr
176, 182, 250, 259, 297, 314, 322

Bedmar & Shi (Singapore)
www.bedmar-and-shi.com
27, 81, 115, 118, 126–27, 202, 356

Steve Blatz (New York)
www.blatzarc.com
43, 167, 238, 289

Bloc Design (Queensland)
www.blocdesign.com.au
23, 82, 279, 330, 342

Bonetti/Kozerski Studio
(New York)
www.bonettikozerski.com
12, 17, 79, 88, 161, 284, 312

Brasil Arquitetura (São Paolo)
www.brasilarq.com.br
79, 117, 136, 142, 259, 311, 313, 325

Mario Caetano (Belo Horizonte,
Brazil)
mario@mariocaetano.com
68, 117, 331

Callas Shortridge Architects
(Culver City, USA)
www.callas-shortridge.com
81, 141, 310, 342

Carole Katleman Interiors
(Los Angeles)
carolekatleman@roadrunner.com
7, 44, 67, 158, 217, 239, 254, 255,
259, 271, 299, 305, 321, 333

Casey Brown Architecture
(Sydney)
www.caseybrown.com.au
228, 264

Chang Architects (Singapore)
www.changarch.com
168

Chu + Gooding (Los Angeles)
www.cg-arch.com
131, 285, 323, 337

**Fernanda Marques
Arquitectos** (São Paolo)
www.fernandamarques.com.br
52

Clive Wilkinson Architects
(Los Angeles)
www.clivewilkinson.com
65, 142, 283

Collett–Zarzycki Ltd (London)
www.collett-zarzycki.com
85, 123, 155, 194, 208, 332

Chris Connell (Victoria, Australia)
www.chrisconnell.com.au
151, 183

Dan Cuevas
cuevasdesigns@sbcglobal.net
44, 67, 217, 239, 254, 255, 259, 299

Albano Daminato (Singapore)
www.albanodaminato.com
182, 190, 297, 311, 324

Channa Daswatte (Sri Lanka)
www.micda.com
85, 102, 169, 217

**David Langston-Jones
Architect** (Sydney)
www.davidlangston-jones.com.au
171, 186, 218, 235, 236

Denton Corker Marshall
(Melbourne)
www.dentoncorkermarshall.com
218, 261

Design King (Sydney)
www.designking.com.au
6, 11, 15, 43, 132, 145, 151, 268, 288

**Dietrich | Untertrifaller
Architekten** (Switzerland)
www.dietrich.untertrifaller.com
33, 83, 124

Donovan Hill (Brisbane)
www.donovanhill.com.au
108, 166, 259, 261, 278, 363

DOS Architects (London)
www.dosarchitects.com
76, 80, 193, 195, 203, 273, 275, 315

DXB Lab (Dubai)
www.dxb-lab.com
20, 45, 179, 276

Eckersley Garden Architecture
(Richmond, Australia)
www.e-ga.com.au
27, 47, 220, 221, 303, 314, 317,
331, 333

Eldridge Smerin (London)
www.eldridgesmerin.com
13, 53, 100, 114, 118, 120, 133,
134, 135, 156, 181, 261

Elizabeth Leong Architects
(Sydney)
www.elarchitects.com.au
7, 16, 211, 224, 292

Gérard Faivre (Paris)
www.gerardfaivreparis.com
43, 46, 84, 90, 142, 147, 149,
161, 195, 219, 236, 277, 278,
294, 318, 334, 336, 337, 344,
355, 358, 359

**Fernanda Marques
Arquitectos** (São Paolo)
www.fernandamarques.com.br
52

Flaunt ID (Auckland)
www.flaunt-id.com
43, 77, 215, 302

Gerrad Hall Architects
(Auckland)
www.gerradhallarchitects.co.nz
11, 128, 129, 140, 168

Greg Natale Design (Sydney)
www.gregnatale.com
60, 76, 155, 196, 200, 244, 245,
270, 297

Meire Gomide
meirebgn@terra.com.br
192, 244

Kevin Haley (Los Angeles)
www.kevinhaley.com
43, 346

Hecker Phelan Guthrie
(Richmond, Australia)
www.hpg.net.au
91, 136, 137

Isay Weinfeld Arquiteto
(São Paolo)
www.isayweinfeld.com
7, 38, 43, 80, 100, 124, 136, 154,
170, 171, 175, 210, 217, 230,
236, 238, 256, 260, 318, 344,
347, 354

James Gorst Architects Ltd
(London)
www.jamesgorstarchitects.com
13, 121

James Russell Architect
(Fortitude Valley, Australia)
www.jamesrussellarchitect.com.au
105, 209, 278, 339

**John Friedman Alice Kimm
Architects** (Los Angeles)
www.jfak.net
167, 212

John Pardey Architects
(Lymington, UK)
www.johnpardeyarchitects.com
124, 151, 174

Kay Kollar Design (Los Angeles)
www.kaykollardesign.com
59, 68, 81, 131, 141, 285, 310,
323, 337, 342

Kerry Hill Architects
(Singapore)
www.kerryhillarchitects.com
79, 217, 224–5, 341, 358

Sharon Kubale
kubale@bigpond.com
151, 183

Rasmus Larsson (Copenhagen)
www.design-by-us.com
65, 124, 151, 166, 217, 268, 270,
355

Leeton Pointon Architects
(Melbourne)
www.leetonpointon.com
79, 118, 119, 155, 260, 266, 265

Lehm Ton Erde (Schlins, Austria)
www.lehmtonerde.at
118, 149, 169, 228, 265

LOH Architects (Culver City,
USA)
www.loharchitects.com
32, 61, 119, 138, 181, 264

Lundberg Design (San
Francisco)
www.lundbergdesign.com
13, 32, 231, 263

Frank Macchia (Queensland)
www.frankmacchia.com
29, 65, 93, 102, 105, 145, 195,
228, 257, 293, 342, 352

Jason Maclean (London)
www.macleaninteriors.com
162, 245, 252–53, 290–91, 335

Marmol Radziner + Associates
(Los Angeles)
www.marmol-radziner.com
6, 11, 12, 21, 30–31, 69, 73, 79,
81, 97, 98–99, 104, 105, 109,
110, 112–13, 114, 117, 144,
146, 150, 166, 217, 223, 228,
299, 304, 306, 329, 330, 345,
346, 357

MELD Architecture (London)
www.meldarchitecture.com
79, 227, 236, 287, 298

Ministry of Design (Singapore)
www.modonline.com
181, 286, 297

**Modern Architectural Practice
Ltd** (London)
www.m-ap.com
139, 226, 303, 304, 307

MXA Development (Venice,
USA)
www.redbarnprefab.com
347

Nathan Egan Interiors
(New York)
www.nathanegan.com
168, 195, 217, 251, 272, 281

NoxonGiffen (Sydney)
www.noxongiffen.com
37, 150, 219

Ruy Ohtake (São Paolo)
www.ruyohtake.com.br
157, 232, 237, 334

Todd Oldham (New York)
www.toddoldhamstudio.com
11, 22, 25, 27, 114, 142, 186,
347, 352

Peter Gluck and Partners
(New York)
www.gluckpartners.com
44, 119, 140, 286, 326, 327

Philip Lutz Architektur
(Lochan, Austria)
www.philiplutz.at
124, 182, 214, 319, 329

Karim Rashid (New York)
www.karimrashid.com
45, 202, 207, 233, 244, 260, 270,
298, 300, 301, 305

Rios Clementi Hale Studios
(Los Angeles)
www.rchstudios.com
85, 178, 186, 219, 228, 224, 245,
358

**Robertson & Hindmarsh
Architects** (Sydney)
www.robertsonandhindmarsh.com.au
24, 57, 294

John Rocha (Dublin)
www.johnrocha.ie
45, 100, 169, 184, 242, 247, 265,
272, 320, 339, 347

Paulo Mendes da Rocha
(São Paolo)
pmr@sti.com.br
45, 169, 247, 265

**Scott Weston Architecture
Design** (Redfern, Australia)
www.swad.com.au
149, 167

Sebastian Mariscal Studio
(San Diego)
www.sebastianmariscal.com
79, 124, 188–89, 226, 274, 325

Sharon Fraser Architects (New
South Wales, Australia)
www.sharonfraserarchitects.com.au
36, 333, 337

Studio Arthur Casas
(São Paolo)
www.arthurcasas.com
1, 9, 11, 12, 56, 106–7, 171, 183,
222, 324, 329, 351, 355

StudioMDA (New York)
www.studiomda.com
45, 88, 158, 181, 241, 246, 259,
297, 308, 313

Studio mk27 (São Paolo)
www.marciokogan.com.br
55, 86–87, 91, 101, 117, 124,
157, 185, 186, 191, 218, 264,
269, 311, 330, 352, 360–61

Susan Minter Design (London)
www.susanminter.com
167, 229, 259, 284, 359

Syntax Lab (Los Angeles)
www.syntax-lab.com
168, 172, 227

**Techentin Buckingham
Architecture** (Los Angeles)
www.techbuckarch.com
66, 175, 244, 305

Temple Home (Los Angeles)
www.templehome.net
85, 229

**Tonkin Zulaikha Greer
Architects** (Sydney)
www.tzg.com.au
26, 94, 338

Tony Owen Partners (Sydney)
www.tonyowen.com.au
288, 293

Toshiko Mori Architect
(New York)
www.tmarch.com
44, 111, 171, 305

Zrinka Twingler (Antibes,
France)
www.zrinkatwingler.com
243

Kim Utzon (Copenhagen)
www.kimutzon.dk
35, 123, 177, 244, 278

Ghislaine Viñas (New York)
www.gvinteriors.com
217, 233, 272, 288, 297, 350

W and R Design (Los Angeles)
www.wandrdesign.com
160

Webb Architects Ltd (London)
www.webb-architects.co.uk
109, 149, 157, 167, 228, 314

Mary Wilson
mary@tllc.com.au
68, 228, 318

WoHa (Singapore)
www.woha-architects.com
117, 130

Xten Architecture (Los Angeles)
www.xtenarchitecture.com
75, 76, 293, 355, 359

retailers

UK

LONDON

Aram Store
110 Drury Lane
London WC2B 5SG
Tel: +44 (0) 20 7557 7557
aramstore@aram.co.uk
www.aram.co.uk

Aria
Barnsbury Hall
Barnsbury Street
London N1 1PN
Tel: +44 (0) 20 7704 1999
ariashop@ariashop.co.uk
www.ariashop.co.uk

The Conran Shop Chelsea
Michelin House,
81 Fulham Road
London SW3 6RD
Tel: +44 (0) 20 7589 7401
fulham@conran.com
www.conran.com

The Conran Shop Marylebone
55 Marylebone High Street
London W1U 5HS
Tel: +44 (0) 20 7723 2223
marylebone@conran.com
www.conran.com

David Phillips Design Classics
The Light Box, 111 Power Road
London W4 5PY
Tel: +44 (0) 845 371 1288
sales@designclassics.co.uk
www.designclassics.co.uk

Geoffrey Drayton
85 Hampstead Road
London NW1 2PL
Tel: +44 (0) 20 7387 5840
enquiries@geoffrey-drayton.co.uk
www.geoffrey-drayton.co.uk

Heal's
196 Tottenham Court Road
London W1T 7LQ
Tel: +44 (0) 20 7636 1666
TCRreception@heals.co.uk
www.heals.co.uk

Ligne Roset
23/25 Mortimer Street
London W1T 3JE
Tel: +44 (0) 20 7323 1248
enquiries@ligne-roset-
westend.co.uk
www.ligne-roset.co.uk

Mint
2 North Terrace
London SW3 2BA
Tel: +44 (0) 20 7225 2228
info@mintshop.co.uk
www.mintshop.co.uk

Places and Spaces
30 Old Town
London SE4 0LB
Tel: +44 (0) 20 7498 0998
contact@placesandspaces.com
www.placesandspaces.com

Skandium
86 Marylebone High Street
London W1U 4QS
Tel: +44 (0) 20 7935 2077
marylebone@skandium.com
www.skandium.com

SCP Ltd
135–139 Curtain Road
London EC2A 3BX
Tel: +44 (0) 20 7739 1869
production@scp.co.uk
www.scp.co.uk

Twentytwentyone
274 Upper Street
London N1 2UA
Tel: +44 (0) 20 7288 1996
shop@twentytwentyone.com
www.twentytwentyone.com

TYE+CO
39 Morpeth Road
London, E9 7LD
Tel: +44 (0) 20 8533 1001
info@tye3d.com
www.tyeandco.com

Vitra Ltd
30 Clerkenwell Road
London EC1M 5PQ
Tel: +44 (0) 20 7608 6200
www.vitra.com

REST OF COUNTRY

A. R. Stockton Ltd
140 Great Ancoats Street
Manchester M4 6DU
Tel: +44 (0) 161 273 5331
sales@stocktons.co.uk
www.stocktons.co.uk

Design Shop
116 Causewayside
Edinburgh EH9 1PU
Tel: +44 (0) 131 667 7078
info@designshopuk.com
www.designshopuk.com

Ferrious
Arch 61, Withworth Street West
Manchester M1 5WQ
Tel: +44 (0) 161 228 6880
enquiries@ferrious.com
www.ferrious.com

The Lollipop Shoppe
44 Trafalgar Street, Brighton
East Sussex BN1 4ED
Tel: +44 (0) 1273 699 119
info@thelollipopshoppe.co.uk
www.thelollipopshoppe.co.uk

Moleta Munro
4 Jeffrey Street
Edinburgh EH1 1DT
Tel: +44 (0) 131 557 4800
info@moletamunro.com
www.moletamunro.com

Rume
54 Western Road, Hove
East Sussex BN3 1JD
Tel: +44 (0) 1273 777 810
info@rume.co.uk
www.rume.co.uk

Utility
60 Bold Street
Liverpool, L1 4EA
Tel: +44 (0) 151 708 4192
info@utilitydesign.co.uk
www.utilitydesign.co.uk

USA

NEW YORK

Auto
805 Washington Street
New York, NY 10014
Tel: +1 212 229 2292
shop@thisisauto.com
www.thisisauto.com

The Conran Shop
407 East 59th Street
New York, NY 10022
Tel: +1 212 755 90 79
www.conran.com

DDC
181 Madison Ave
New York, NY 10016
Tel: +1 212 685 0800
info@ddcnyc.com
www.ddcnyc.com

Design Within Reach
142 Wooster Street
New York, NY 10012
Tel: +1 212 471 0280
soho@dwr.com
www.dwr.com

The Future Perfect
115 North 6th Street
New York, NY 11211
Tel: +1 718 599 6278
info@thefutureperfect.com
www.thefutureperfect.com

I Heart
262 Mott Street
New York, NY 10012
Tel: +1 212 219 9265
www.thingsweheart@
blogspot.com

The Karim Rashid Shop
137 West 19th Street
New York, NY 10011
Tel: +1 212 337 8078
office@karimrashid.com
www.karimrashid.com

Lee's Studio
220 West 57th Street
New York, NY 10019
Tel: +1 212 247 0110
sales@leesstudio.com
www.leesstudio.com

Ligne Roset Midtown
250 Park Avenue South
New York, NY 10003
Tel: +1 212 375 1036
www.lignerosetny.com

Ligne Roset SoHo
155 Wooster Street
New York, NY 10012
Tel: +1 212 253 5629
www.lignerosetny.com

Matter
405 Broome Street
New York, NY 10013
Tel: +1 212 343 2600
info@mattermatters.com
www.mattermatters.com

Mies Design Shop
319 West 47th Street
New York, NY 10036
Tel: +1 212 247 3132

MoMA Design Store
11 West 53rd Street
New York, NY 10036
Tel: +1 212 708 9700
feedback@moma.org
www.momastore.org

Moss
150 Greene Street
New York, NY 10012
Tel: +1 212 204 7100
store@mossonline.com
www.mossonline.com

The Vitra Store
29 9th Avenue
New York, NY 10014
Tel: +1 212 463 5700
www.vitra.com

LOS ANGELES

Diva
8815 Beverly Boulevard
Los Angeles, CA 90048
Tel: +1 310 278 3191
info@divafurniture.com
www.divafurniture.com

Eames Office Gallery
850 Pico Boulevard
Santa Monica, CA 90405
Tel: +1 310 396 5991
gallery@eamesgallery.com
www.eamesgallery.com

Lawson-Fenning
7257 Beverly Boulevard
Los Angeles, CA 90036
Tel: +1 323 934 0048
info@lawsonfenning.com
www.lawsonfenning.com

Modernica
7366 Beverly Boulevard
Los Angeles, CA 90036
Tel: +1 323 933 0383
lashowroom@modernica.net
www.modernica.net

Twentieth
8057 Beverly Boulevard
Los Angeles, CA 90048
Tel: +1 323 9041 200
info@twentieth.net
www.twentieth.net

SAN FRANCISCO

Arkitektura
560 9th Street
San Francisco, CA 94103
Tel: +1 415-565-7200
sales@arksf.com
www.arksf.com

Dzine
128 Utah Street
San Francisco, CA 94103
Tel: +1 415 674 9430
info@dzinestore.com
www.dzinestore.com

AUSTRALIA

Angelucci 20th Century
92 High Street
Windsor, Victoria 3181
Tel: +61 (0) 3 9525 1271
info@angelucci.net.au
www.angelucci.net.au

Anibou
726 Bourke Street
Redfern, NSW 2016
Tel: +61 (0) 2 9319 0655
syd@anibou.com.au
www.anibou.com.au

Hub Sydney
66–72 Reservoir Street
Surry Hills, NSW 2010
Tel +61 (0) 2 9217 0700
info@hubfurniture.com.au
www.hubfurniture.com.au

Ken Neale Twentieth Century Modern
3/138 Darlinghurst Rd,
Darlinghurst, NSW 2010
Tel: + 61 (0) 410 463 121

KE-ZU
61 Marlborough Street
Surry Hills, NSW 2010
Tel: +61 (0) 2 9699 6600
www.kezu.com.au

Living Edge Studio
74 Commonwealth Street
Surry Hills, NSW 2010
Tel: +61 (0) 2 9640 5600
sydneysales@livingedge.com.au
www.livingedge.com.au

Make Designed Objects
194 Elgin Street
Carlton, Victoria 3053
Tel: +61 (0) 3 9347 4225
info@makedesignedobjects.com
www.makedesignedobjects.com

picture references

All numbers in bold refer to page numbers.

1 Cool Modernism prevails in a house in southern Brazil with glass walls that make the jungle part of the interior.
3 A double-height space in a modern New Zealand residence is both light and efficient with two storeys of windows and a soaring wall of books.
14–15 Houses inspired by the International Style, with glass walls and overhanging roof, are adapted to the forest of the Blue Mountains, Australia (left) and the open shoreline of Palm Beach, Florida (right).
46–47 A Provençal house filled with iconic furniture and sculptural pieces, and a cottage on the Mornington Peninsula, Australia, marry rustic charm with modern flair.
82–83 Indoor–outdoor living spaces in a forested Australian setting (left) and in the less temperate environs of Austria (right) demonstrate that climate does not always determine lifestyle.
120 Modern style and materials in a striking new house in parkland outside of London. The transparent wall makes the abundant greenery part of the interior.
121 Another UK residence creates a dramatic and more enclosed atmosphere with dark wood and highly polished flooring.
152–53 Metal panels brighten the exterior of a California house while mossy stone and intricately carved wood form a backdrop for modern living in Bali.
184–85 White minimalist purity is warmed by contrasting dark wood elements in John Rocha's French retreat while a more polished kind of minimalism holds sway in a new Brazilian design.
220–21 Colour is not just an internal affair in this bold design for a holiday cottage in Australia. The rustic metal siding and flagstone floors have become part of a bright modern palette.
262–63 Natural light and rough-hewn wood are some of the traditional ingredients for a cosy rural retreat updated here in Chile (left) and northern California, in a clean modern manner.
300–1 Against a backdrop as vibrant as that of designer Karim Rashid's interiors, furniture needs strong shape and colour of its own, such as the solid, sculptural forms of his variation of his own Kurve chair (left) and Swing chair (right).
332–23 New approaches to garden spaces in the UK (left), where the humble cut log becomes a work of art, and in Austalia (right), where a sculpture park can be your own backyard.

LOCATIONS & ACKNOWLEDGMENTS

Key:
– Location is given, followed by the principal designer or architect, or owner. Designers and architects are also listed on p. 364.
– All images listed from left to right, or clockwise from top left.

1 Brazil / Studio Arthur Casas. **2** New Zealand / Andrew Lister Architect. **6** USA / Marmol Radziner; UK / Ban Shubber Associates; Australia / Jon King, Design King Company (architect), Stephen Collins (designer). **7** Brazil / Isay Weinfeld Arquiteto; USA / Carole Katleman Interiors; Australia / Elizabeth Leong Architects. **8** Turkey / Murat Patavi, www.republicaadv.com; USA / n/a; Australia / Glenn Murcutt. **9** USA / Barton Myers Associates; Sri Lanka / Anjalendran C. Architect; Brazil / Studio Arthur Casas. **11** (top) New Zealand / Gerrad Hall; USA / Marmol Radziner; USA / Todd Oldham; (middle) Australia / Glenn Murcutt; Australia / Jon King, Design King Company (architect), Stephen Collins (designer) USA / Albert Frey, www.psmuseum.org; (bottom): Brazil / Studio Arthur Casas. **12** Australia / Jenny Kee, www.jennykee.com / Glenn Murcutt; Brazil / Studio Arthur Casas; USA / John Lautner / Marmol Radziner; USA / Bonetti/Kozerski / Studio Donna Karan International, www.dkny.com.
13 USA / Aleks Istanbullu Architects; USA / Lundberg Design; UK / James Gorst Architects; UK / Eldridge Smerin. **14** Australia / Glenn Murcutt. **15** Australia / Jon King, Design King (architect), Stephen Collins (designer).
16 Australia / Elizabeth Leong Architects. **17** USA / Bonetti/Kozerski Studio / Studio Donna Karan International, www.dkny.com. **18–19** USA / Albert Frey, www.psmuseum.org. **20** Dubai / Khalid al Najjar, DXB Lab.
21 USA / Marmol Radziner. **22** USA / Todd Oldham; Australia / Jenny Kee, www.jennykee.com. **23** Australia / Bark Design Architects; Australia / Bloc Design. **24** Australia / Robertson & Hindmarsh Architects. **25** USA / Todd Oldham. **26** Australia / Brian Zulaikha, Tonkin Zulaikha Greer Architects. **27** (clockwise) Singapore / Ernesto Bedmar, Bedmar & Shi; Switzerland / Bauart Architekten und Planer/ Living Etc/IPC+ Syndication; USA / Todd Oldham; Australia / Eckersley Garden Architecture.
28 USA / Barton Myers Associates. **29** Australia / Frank Macchia. **30–31** USA / John Lautner / Marmol Radziner.
32 USA / Lundberg Design; USA / LOH Architects.
33 Austria / Dietrich | Untertrifaller Architekten.
34 Australia / Glenn Murcutt. **35** Denmark / Kim Utzon.
36 (both images) Australia / Sharon Fraser Architects.
37 Australia / NoxonGiffen Architects; Australia / Denton Corker Marshall. **38** Brazil / Isay Weinfeld. **39** Brazil / Studio mk27. **40–41** (both images) Bali / AREA Designs.

43 (top) Brazil / Isay Weinfeld; USA / Steve Blatz, courtesy Collection Olivier Renaud-Clement, New York; Turkey / Murat Patavi, www.republicaadv.com; (middle) France / Gérard Faivre; USA / Kevin Haley; Australia / Jon King, Design King (architect), Stephen Collins (designer); (bottom) New Zealand / Flaunt ID. **44** UK / Carole Katleman Interiors and Dan Cuevas; USA / Toshiko Mori Architect; USA /Mies van der Rohe / Peter Gluck and Partners; Denmark / Vipp, www.vipp.com. **45** USA / Markus Dochantschi, StudioMDA / Jonny Detiger, www.jonnydetiger.com; USA / Karim Rashid; Dubai / Khalid al Najjar, DXB Lab; Brazil / Paulo Mendes da Rocha, www.galerialeme.com. **46** France / Gérard Faivre.
47 Australia / Eckersley Garden Architecture.
48 (both images) Chile / Magdalena Bernstein Architect.
49 Chile / Magdalena Bernstein. **50** UK / Antoni Burakowski & Kerry Warn, www.antoniandalison.co.uk.
51 UK / Antoni Burakowski & Kerry Warn, www.antoniandalison.co.uk. **52** Brazil / Fernanda Marques Arquitectos; France / Eric Allart. **53** UK / Eldridge Smerin.
54 UK / Ban Shubber Associates. **55** (top) Australia / Elizabeth Leong; (bottom) Brazil / Studio mk27. **56** Brazil / Studio Arthur Casas. **57** Australia / Robertson & Hindmarsh. **58** USA / Michael Sainato and Iris in 't Hout, www.bigtreedesign.com, www.extrasmall.com.
59 USA / Kay Kollar Design. **60** (top) USA / n/a; Australia / Greg Natale Design; Australia / Greg Natale; (bottom) Switzerland / AFGH; USA / John Lautner / Brent Bolthouse, www.bolthouseproductions.com; USA / n/a.
61 USA / LOH Architects. **62** USA / Adam Silverman, www.heathceramics.com. **63** (both) USA / Adam Silverman, www.heathceramics.com. **64** USA / Sue Hostetler, www.hostetler.com. **65** (clockwise) Denmark / Jakob Blom; Australia / Frank Macchia; Denmark / Rasmus Larsson; USA / Clive Wilkinson Architects. **66** USA / Techentin Buckingham Architecture. **67** UK / Carole Katleman Interiors and Dan Cuevas. **68** (top) Australia / Giovanni d'Ercole, www.loveandhatred.com.au; USA / Kay Kollar Design; Sri Lanka / George Cooper, www.kahandakanda.com; (bottom) Australia / Mary Wilson; Brazil / Mario Caetano, www.passadocomposto.com.br; Australia / Jenny Kee, www.jennykee.com. **69** USA / Marmol Radziner; Sri Lanka / Jack & Jo Eden, www.villasinsrilanka.com, www.joedenmimimango.com.
70 USA / Michael Sainato and Iris in 't Hout, www.bigtreedesign.com, www.extrasmall.com; USA / Glenn Lawson and Grant Fenning, www.lawsonfenning.com. **71** USA/ Richard Neutra, www.paoutdoor.com.
72 Denmark / n/a. **73** USA / Marmol Radziner. **74** Brazil / Charles Cosac, www.cosacnaify.com.br. **75** USA / Xten Architecture / Randolph Duke, www.randolphduke.com.
76 (clockwise) USA / Xten Architecture / Randolph Duke, www.randolphduke.com; UK / Antoni Burakowski & Kerry Warn, www.antoniandalison.co.uk; Australia / Greg Natale; UK / DOS Architects. **77** New Zealand / Flaunt ID.

79 (top) Brazil / Marcelo Ferraz, Brasil Arquitetura; USA / Sebastian Mariscal Studio; USA / Aleks Istanbullu; (middle) USA / Bonetti/Kozerski Studio / Studio Donna Karan International, www.dkny.com; Singapore / Kerry Hill Architects; USA / John Lautner / Marmol Radziner; (bottom) Australia / Donovan Hill; USA / Marmol Radziner; France / Vicky Thornton and Jef Smith, MELD.
80 Switzerland / AFGH; Brazil / mk27; UK / DOS; Brazil / Isay Weinfeld. **81** USA / Marmol Radziner; USA / Aleks Istanbullu; USA / Kay Kollar Design / Callas Shortridge Architects; Singapore / Ernesto Bedmar, Bedmar & Shi.
82 Australia / Bloc Design. **83** Austria / Dietrich | Untertrifaller. **84** France / Gérard Faivre. **85** (clockwise) Sri Lanka / Channa Daswatte; USA / Lloyd Wright and Temple Home; USA / Rios Clementi Hale Studios; UK / Collett-Zarzycki Ltd. **86–87** Brazil / Studio mk27. **88** (top) USA / Markus Dochantschi, StudioMDA / Jonny Detiger, www.jonnydetiger.com; (bottom) USA / Bonetti/Kozerski Studio / Studio Donna Karan International, www.dkny.com.
89 Denmark / Vipp, www.vipp.com. **90** (top) USA / Adam Silverman, www.heathceramics.com; France / Gérard Faivre; USA / Angie Hill, www.angiehill.com; (middle) Australia / Baker Kavanagh Architects; USA / Amy Finn Bernier Architect ; Australia / n/a; (bottom) France / Gérard Faivre; France / Gérard Faivre; Italy / Damiano Petrioli, www.decortex.com. **91** (clockwise) Brazil / Studio mk27; Australia / Hecker Phelan Guthrie; USA / Aleks Istanbullu; USA / Aleks Istanbullu. **92** USA / n/a; USA / Michael Sainato and Iris in 't Hout, www.bigtreedesign.com, www.extrasmall.com. **93** Australia / Frank Macchia. **94** Australia / Brian Zulaikha, Tonkin Zulaikha Greer. **95** Australia / Donovan Hill.
96 USA / Aleks Istanbullu. **97** USA / Marmol Radziner.
98–99 USA / Marmol Radziner. **100** (clockwise) UK / Eldridge Smerin; Brazil / Isay Weinfeld; France / John Rocha. **101** Brazil / Studio mk27. **102** Sri Lanka / Channa Daswatte; Australia / Frank Macchia. **103** Australia / Bark Design. **104** Australia / Frank Macchia. **105** (clockwise) Australia / Frank Macchia; Australia / Frank Macchia; Australia / James Russell Architect. **106–7** Brazil / Studio Arthur Casas. **108** Australia / Donovan Hill. **109** UK / Webb Architects; USA / Marmol Radziner. **110** USA / John Lautner / Marmol Radziner; USA / John Lautner / Brent Bolthouse, www.bolthouseproductions.com. **111** USA / Toshiko Mori. **112–13** USA / John Lautner / Marmol Radziner. **114** (clockwise) UK / Eldridge Smerin; USA / John Lautner / Marmol Radziner; USA / Todd Oldham; USA / John Lautner / Marmol Radziner. **115** Singapore / Ernesto Bedmar, Bedmar & Shi.

117 (top) Brazil / Studio mk27; USA / Barton Myers; Singapore / WoHa; (middle) Brazil / Marcelo Ferraz, Brasil Arquitetura; Switzerland / Bauart/ Living Etc/IPC+ Syndication; USA / John Lautner / Marmol Radziner; (bottom) New Zealand / Andrew Lister; Brazil / Mario Caetano, www.passadocomposto.com.br. **118** Austria / Lehm Ton Erde; Singapore / Ernesto Bedmar, Bedmar & Shi; Australia / Leeton Pointon Architects; UK / Eldridge Smerin. **119** USA / LOH Architects; Australia / Donovan Hill; Australia / Leeton Pointon Architects; USA / Mies van der Rohe / Peter Gluck and Partners. **120** UK / Eldridge Smerin. **121** UK / James Gorst. **122** Chile / Magdalena Bernstein. **123** UK / Collett-Zarzycki; Denmark / Kim Utzon. **124** (top) Austria / Philip Lutz Architektur; Brazil / Isay Weinfeld; Denmark / Rasmus Larsson; (middle) Brazil / Studio mk27; USA / Sebastian Mariscal; USA / John Lautner / Brent Bolthouse, www.bolthouseproductions.com; (bottom) Austria / Dietrich | Untertrifaller; UK / John Pardey Architects; Brazil / Isay Weinfeld. **125** Australia / Kerry and Lindsay Clare, Architectus. **126–27** Singapore / Ernesto Bedmar, Bedmar & Shi. **128** (both images) New Zealand / Gerrad Hall. **129** New Zealand / Gerrad Hall. **130** Singapore / WoHa. **131** USA / Kay Kollar Design / Chu + Gooding Architects. **132** Australia / Jon King, Design King (architect), Stephen Collins (designer). **133** UK / Eldridge Smerin. **134** UK / Eldridge Smerin. **135** UK / Eldridge Smerin. **136** (clockwise) Brazil / Marcelo Ferraz, Brasil Arquitetura; Australia / Hecker Phelan Guthrie; Brazil / Isay Weinfeld. **137** Australia / Hecker Phelan Guthrie. **138** USA / LOH Architects. **139** UK / Modern Architectural Practice.
140 USA / Mies van der Rohe / Peter Gluck and Partners; New Zealand / Gerrad Hall. **141** USA / Kay Kollar Design / Callas Shortridge; Bali / AREA. **142** (clockwise) USA / Living Etc/IPC+ Syndication; Australia / Giovanni d'Ercole, www.loveandhatred.com.au; Brazil / Marcelo Ferraz, Brasil Arquitetura; France / Gérard Faivre; USA / Todd Oldham; USA / Clive Wilkinson. **143** Brazil / Studio mk27; USA / Albert Frey, www.psmuseum.org. **144** USA / Marmol Radziner; (right) UK / Antoni Burakowski and Kerry Warn www.antoniandalison.co.uk. **145** Australia / Frank Macchia; Australia / Jon King, Design King Company.
146 (clockwise) Bali / AREA; UK / Antoni Burakowski and Kerry Warn www.antoniandalison.co.uk; Italy / Damiano Petrioli, www.decortex.com; USA / Marmol Radziner.
147 France / Gérard Faivre.

149 (top) UK / Webb; France / Gérard Faivre; Denmark/ n/a; (middle) Australia / Scott Weston Architecture Design; UK / Webb; Australia / Kerry and Lindsay Clare, Architectus; (bottom) USA / Steve Shaw, www.steveshawphotography.com. **150** USA / Marmol Radziner; Austria / Lehm Ton Erde; USA / John Lautner / Marmol Radziner; Australia / NoxonGiffen. **151** UK / John Pardey; Denmark / Rasmus Larsson; Australia / Jon King, Design King Company; Australia / Chris Connell and Sharon Kubale.
152 USA / Aleks Istanbullu. **153** Bali / AREA. **154** Brazil / Isay Weinfeld; Sri Lanka / Anjalendran C. Architect.
155 (top) UK / Collett-Zarzycki; (bottom) Australia / Greg Natale; Australia / Leeton Pointon; Sri Lanka / n/a.
156 UK / Eldridge Smerin. **157** (clockwise) Brazil / Studio mk27; Brazil / Ruy Ohtake; UK / Webb. **158** USA / Carole Katleman Interiors. **159** USA / Markus Dochantschi, StudioMDA / Jonny Detiger, www.jonnydetiger.com.
160 USA / W and R Design. **161** (clockwise) USA / Bonetti/Kozerski Studio / Studio Donna Karan International, www.dkny.com; USA / Heath Ceramics, www.heathceramics.com; Italy / Damiano Petrioli, www.decortex.com; France / Gérard Faivre; Italy / Damiano Petrioli, www.decortex.com; France / Gérard Faivre. **162** France / Jason Maclean. **163** USA / Adam Silverman, www.heathceramics.com. **164** UK / Antoni Burakowski and Kerry Warn, www.antoniandalison.co.uk.
165 Turkey / Autoban. **166** (clockwise) USA / John

Lautner / Marmol Radziner; Switzerland / AFGH; Australia / Donovan Hill; Denmark / Rasmus Larsson.
167 (top) Australia / Scott Weston; USA / Susan Minter Design; (bottom left) USA / Amy Finn Bernier; (clockwise from centre) USA / Heath Ceramics, www.heathceramics.com; USA / Steve Blatz, courtesy collection Olivier Renaud-Clement, New York; USA / John Friedman Alice Kimm Architects; UK / Webb.
168 (clockwise) USA / Steffen Leisner, Ali Jeevanjee, Phillip Trigas, Syntax Lab; USA / Nathan Egan Interiors; New Zealand / Gerrad Hall; Singapore / Chang Architects.
169 (clockwise from top) Austria / Lehm Ton Erde; Sri Lanka / Channa Daswatte; Brazil / Paulo Mendes da Rocha, www.galerialeme.com. **170** Brazil / Isay Weinfeld.
171 (top left, clockwise) Brazil / Isay Weinfeld; Italy / Agape Design; Brazil / Studio Arthur Casas; Australia / David Langston-Jones Architect; (top right) Australia / Jenny Kee, www.jennykee.com; (bottom right) USA / Toshiko Mori; (bottom left) USA / Heath Ceramics, www.heathceramics.com. **172** USA / Steffen Leisner, Ali Jeevanjee, Phillip Trigas, Syntax Lab. **173** UK / Ban Shubber. **174** UK / John Pardey; Denmark / n/a.
175 Brazil / Isay Weinfeld; USA / Techentin Buckingham.
176 France / Florence Baudoux. **177** Denmark / Kim Utzon. **178** USA / Rios Clementi Hale; UK / James Gorst.
179 Dubai / Khalid al Najjar, DXB Lab; UK / James Gorst.

181 (top) UK / Eldridge Smerin; USA / Michael Sainato and Iris in 't Hout, www.bigtreedesign.com, www.extrasmall.com; USA / LOH Architects; (middle) Brazil / Charles Cosac, www.cosacnaify.com.br; USA / Markus Dochantschi, StudioMDA / Jonny Detiger, www.jonnydetiger.com; Singapore / Ministry of Design; (bottom) Australia / Ministry of Design. **182** Austria / Philip Lutz; Singapore / Albano Daminato; France / Florence Baudoux; USA / Michael Sainato and Iris in 't Hout, www.bigtreedesign.com, www.extrasmall.com. **183** Turkey / Murat Patavi, www.republicaadv.com; Australia / Glenn Murcutt; Australia / Chris Connell and Sharon Kubale; Brazil / Studio Arthur Casas. **184** France / John Rocha.
185 Brazil / Studio mk27. **186** (top) USA / Rios Clementi Hale; USA / Warner Walcott, warner@artrepteam.com; Australia / David Langston-Jones (bottom) USA / Aleks Istanbullu; Brazil / Studio mk27; USA / Todd Oldham.
187 Switzerland / AFGH. **188–89** USA / Sebastian Mariscal. **190** Singapore / Albano Daminato.
191 Brazil / Studio mk27. **192** Brazil / Meire Gomide, www.passadocomposto.com.br. **193** UK / DOS; (right) USA / Amy Finn Bernier. **194** UK / Collett-Zarzycki.
195 (top) France / Gérard Faivre; UK / DOS; (bottom) Australia / Frank Macchia; USA / Nathan Egan; France / Vivian Fraser Architect. **196** Australia / Greg Natale; [illegible] **197** [illegible]
198 USA / Michael Sainato and Iris in 't Hout, www.bigtreedesign.com, www.extrasmall.com.
199 USA / Heath Ceramics, www.heathceramics.com.
200 Australia / Greg Natale. **201** USA / Barton Myers.
202 USA / Karim Rashid; Singapore / Ernesto Bedmar, Bedmar & Shi. **203** UK / DOS **204** UK / James Gorst.
205 USA / Sue Hostetler, www.hostetler.com.
206 Chile / Magdalena Bernstein; USA / Adam Silverman, www.heathceramics.com. **207** Denmark / n/a; USA / Karim Rashid. **208** Chile / Magdalena Bernstein; UK / Collett-Zarzycki. **209** Australia / James Russell. **210** Brazil / Isay Weinfeld. **211** Australia / Elizabeth Leong; Turkey / Murat Patavi, www.republicaadv.com. **212** USA / John Friedman Alice Kimm. **213** UK / James Gorst.
214 (clockwise) Turkey / Murat Patavi, www.republicaadv.com; Austria / Philip Lutz; Australia / n/a; USA / Barton Myers. **215** New Zealand / Flaunt ID.

217 (top) Singapore / Kerry Hill; Sri Lanka / Channa Daswatte; Brazil / Isay Weinfeld; (middle) USA / Ghislaine Viñas; UK / Carole Katleman Interiors and Dan Cuevas; USA / Nathan Egan; (bottom) USA / Marmol Radziner; Denmark / Rasmus Larrsson. **218** Australia / David Langston-Jones; USA / Barton Myers.; Australia / Denton Corker Marshall; Brazil / Studio mk27. **219** Singapore / Kerry Hill; France / Gérard Faivre; Australia / NoxonGiffen; USA / Rios Clementi Hale. **220** Australia / Eckersley Garden Architecture. **221** Australia / Eckersley Garden Architecture. **222** Brazil / Studio Arthur Casas.
223 (both images) USA / Marmol Radziner.
224 (left) Australia / Elizabeth Leong. **224–25** Singapore / Kerry Hill. **226** UK / Modern Architectural Practice; USA / Sebastian Mariscal. **227** USA / Steffen Leisner, Ali Jeevanjee, Phillip Trigas, Syntax Lab; Brazil / Charles Cosac, www.cosacnaify.com.br. **228** (top) Australia / Frank Macchia; USA / Rios Clementi Hale; (bottom right) USA / Marmol Radziner; (clockwise from bottom left) Australia / Mary Wilson; Australia / Casey Brown Architecture; Austria / Lehm Ton Erde; UK / Webb.
229 USA / Lloyd Wright and Temple Home; USA / Susan Minter Design. **230** Brazil / Isay Weinfeld. **231** (clockwise from top) USA / n/a; USA / Lundberg Design; USA / Heath Ceramics, www.heathceramics.com. **232** Brazil / Ruy Ohtake. **233** (top) Denmark / n/a; USA / Ghislaine Viñas; USA / n/a; (bottom) Brazil / Charles Cosac, www.cosacnaify.com.br; Switzerland / AFGH; USA / Karim Rashid. **234** USA / Michael Sainato and Iris in 't Hout, www.bigtreedesign.com, www.extrasmall.com.
235 Australia / David Langston-Jones. **236** (top) USA / Amy Finn Bernier; USA/ Richard Neutra, www.paoutdoor.com; USA / n/a; (middle) UK / Ban Shubber; Australia / David Langston-Jones; Brazil / Isay Weinfeld; (bottom) USA / Amy Finn Bernier; France / Vicky Thornton and Jef Smith, MELD; France / Gérard Faivre.
237 Brazil / Ruy Ohtake. **238** (clockwise) Denmark / Jakob Blom; Switzerland / Bauart / Living Etc/IPC+ Syndication; USA / Steve Blatz / 'sella' chair by Joe Colombo, 1967, courtesy Collection Olivier Renaud-Clement, New York; Brazil / Isay Weinfeld; France / Vivian Fraser; Denmark / Vipp, www.vipp.com. **239** Australia / n/a.
240 USA / Sue Hostetler, www.hostetler.com.
241 USA / Hamilton Design Associates Inc. **242** Denmark / n/a; France / John Rocha. **243** France / Zrinka Twingler, Vice Versa. **244** (top) USA / Michael Sainato and Iris in 't Hout, www.bigtreedesign.com, www.extrasmall.com; Brazil / Meire Gomide, www.passadocomposto.com.br; (middle) Brazil / Meire Gomide; USA / Rios Clementi Hale; USA / Karim Rashid; (bottom) USA / Techentin Buckingham; Australia / Greg Natale; Denmark / Kim Utzon. **245** (clockwise) Australia / Greg Natale; USA / Rios Clementi Hale; France / Jason Maclean.
246 USA / Markus Dochantschi, StudioMDA / Jonny Detiger, www.jonnydetiger.com. **247** Brazil / Paulo Mendes da Rocha, www.galerialeme.com.
248 USA / Warner Walcott, warner@artrepteam.com. **249** [illegible] **250** [illegible] Baudoux. **251** USA / Nathan Egan. **252–53** France / Jason Maclean. **254** UK / Carole Katleman Interiors and Dan Cuevas. **255** Australia / Greg Natale; UK / Carole Katleman Interiors and Dan Cuevas. **256** (clockwise) Brazil / Isay Weinfeld; Brazil / Isay Weinfeld; Brazil / Charles Cosac, www.cosacnaify.com.br. **257** Australia / Frank Macchia.

259 (top) Brazil / Marcelo Ferraz, Brasil Arquitetura; UK / Carole Katleman Interiors and Dan Cuevas; USA / Markus Dochantschi, StudioMDA / Jonny Detiger, www.jonnydetiger.com; (middle) Denmark / Vipp, www.vipp.com; Australia / Donovan Hill; USA / Susan Minter Design; (bottom) France / Florence Baudoux; USA / Assembledge+. **260** Turkey / Murat Patavi, www.republicaadv.com; Brazil / Isay Weinfeld; Australia / Leeton Pointon; USA / Karim Rashid. **261** UK / Eldridge Smerin; Australia / Donovan Hill; Australia / Denton Corker Marshall; Australia / Donovan Hill. **262** Chile; Magdalena Bernstein. **263** USA / Lundberg Design. **264** (clockwise) Australia / Casey Brown Architecture; Brazil / Studio mk27; USA / LOH Architects; Sri Lanka / Anjalendran C. Architect. **265** (clockwise) Brazil / Paulo Mendes da Rocha, www.galerialeme.com; Denmark / Vipp, www.vipp.com; Austria / Lehm Ton Erde.
266 Brazil / Isay Weinfeld. **267** USA / John Lautner / Marmol Radziner. **268** (left) Denmark / Rasmus Larsson; (right) Australia / Jon King, Design King Company.
269 Brazil / Studio mk27. **270** (top) USA / n/a; Denmark / Rasmus Larsson; USA / Karim Rashid; (middle) Australia / Greg Natale; Switzerland / AFGH; France / Eric Allart; (bottom) USA / Karim Rashid; Denmark / Vipp, www.vipp.com; New Zealand / Andrew Lister Architect.
271 USA / Carole Katleman Interiors. **272** (clockwise) USA / Nathan Egan; France / John Rocha; USA / Ghislaine Viñas; France / Gérard Faivre. **273** (both images) UK / DOS. **274** USA / Sebastian Mariscal.
275 UK / DOS **276** Dubai / Khalid al Najjar, DXB Lab.
277 Brazil / Studio mk27. **278** (clockwise) Denmark / Kim Utzon; France / Gérard Faivre; Australia / Donovan Hill; Australia / James Russell. **279** Australia / Bloc Design.
280 USA / Michael Sainato and Iris in 't Hout, www.bigtreedesign.com, www.extrasmall.com.
281 USA / Nathan Egan. **282** USA / Michael Sainato and Iris in 't Hout, www.bigtreedesign.com, www.extrasmall.com. **283** USA / Clive Wilkinson.
284 Switzerland / AFGH; USA / Bonetti/Kozerski / Studio Donna Karan International, www.dkny.com.
285 USA / Kay Kollar Design / Chu + Gooding Architects.
286 (clockwise) Singapore / Ministry of Design; USA / Mies van der Rohe / Peter Gluck and Partners; USA / Michael Sainato and Iris in 't Hout, www.bigtreedesign.com, www.extrasmall.com.
287 France / Vicky Thornton and Jef Smith, MELD.
288 (top) Australia / Tony Owen Partners; Turkey / Autoban; (bottom) Brazil / Charles Cosac, www.cosacnaify.com.br; USA / Ghislaine Viñas; Australia / Jon King, Design King (architect), Stephen Collins (designer). **289** USA / Steve Blatz / Yuichi Higashionna, commissioned in 2007, courtesy Marianne Boesky Gallery, New York.
290–91 France / Jason Maclean. **292** Australia / Elizabeth Leong. **293** (clockwise) USA / Xten Architecture / Randolph Duke, www.randolphduke.com; Australia / Frank Macchia; USA / Steve Shaw, www.steveshawphotography.com; Australia / Tony Owen Partners. **294** (top) USA / n/a; USA / Assembledge+; (clockwise from bottom left) USA / Angie Hill, www.angiehill.com; France / Gérard Faivre; Sri Lanka / George Cooper, www.kahandakanda.com; Australia / Robertson & Hindmarsh. **295** Denmark / Vipp, www.vipp.com.

297 (top) Brazil / Charles Cosac, www.cosacnaify.com.br; USA / Markus Dochantschi, StudioMDA / Jonny Detiger, www.jonnydetiger.com; USA / n/a; (middle) Singapore / Albano Daminato; USA / Ghislaine Viñas; Australia / Greg Natale; (bottom) France / Florence Baudoux [illegible]
298 Brazil / Studio mk27; France / Vicky Thornton and Jef Smith, MELD; Singapore / Ministry of Design; USA / Karim Rashid. **299** UK / Carole Katleman Interiors and Dan Cuevas; Chile / Magdalena Bernstein; USA / Michael Sainato and Iris in 't Hout, www.bigtreedesign.com, www.extrasmall.com; USA / Marmol Radziner. **300** USA / Karim Rashid. **301** USA / Karim Rashid. **302** USA / Richard Neutra, www.paoutdoor.com; New Zealand / Flaunt ID. **303** Australia / Eckersley Garden Architecture; UK / Modern Architectural Practice. **304** (top) UK / Modern Architectural Practice; (bottom) USA / Richard Neutra, www.paoutdoor.com; USA / Warner Walcott, warner@artrepteam.com; USA / John Lautner / Marmol Radziner. **305** (top) USA / Techentin Buckingha.; USA / Carole Katleman Interiors (bottom) USA / Toshiko Mori; Italy / Agape Design; Turkey / Autoban. **306** USA / Marmol Radziner. **307** (left) UK / Modern Architectural Practice; UK / James Gorst. **308** USA / Markus Dochantschi, StudioMDA / Jonny Detiger, www.jonnydetiger.com.
309 USA / Aleks Istanbullu. **310** USA / Kay Kollar Design / Callas Shortridge. **311** (clockwise) USA / n/a; Brazil / Marcelo Ferraz, Brasil Arquitetura; Brazil / Studio mk27; Singapore / Albano Daminato. **312** USA / Bonetti/Kozerski / Studio Donna Karan International, www.dkny.com. **313** USA / Markus Dochantschi, StudioMDA / Jonny Detiger, www.jonnydetiger.com; Brazil / Marcelo Ferraz, Brasil Arquitetura. **314** (clockwise) Australia / Eckersley Garden Architecture; UK / Webb; France / Florence Baudoux; Australia / Jenny Kee, www.jennykee.com. **315** UK / DOS. **316** France / Eric Allart. **317** Sri Lanka / Jack and Jo Eden, www.villasinsrilanka.com, www.joedenmimimango.com; Australia / Eckersley Garden Architecture. **318** (clockwise) France / Gérard Faivre; Australia / Mary Wilson; France / Gérard Faivre; Brazil / Isay Weinfeld. **319** Austria / Philip Lutz. **320** France / John Rocha. **321** USA / Carole Katleman Interiors. **322** France / Florence Baudoux.
323 USA / Kay Kollar Design / Chu + Gooding Architects.
324 Brazil / Studio Arthur Casas; Australia / Albano Daminato. **325** Brazil / Marcelo Ferraz, Brasil Arquitetura; USA / Sebastian Mariscal. **326** USA / Mies van der Rohe / Peter Gluck and Partners. **327** USA / Mies van der Rohe / Peter Gluck and Partners.

329 (top) New Zealand / Andrew Lister; USA / Barton Myers; USA / Barton Myers.; (middle) Australia / Milenko Mijuskovic Architects; Austria / Philip Lutz; Brazil / Studio Arthur Casas; (bottom) [illegible] USA / Marmol Radziner. **330** Brazil / Studio mk27; Australia / Bloc Design; USA / John Lautner / Marmol Radziner; Australia / Keith McCutcheon, www.casaguardi.com. **331** Australia / Eckersley Garden Architecture; Italy / Agape Design; Sri Lanka / George Cooper, www.kahandakanda.com; Brazil / Mario Caetano, www.passadocomposto.com.br.
332 UK / Collett-Zarzycki. **333** Australia / Sharon Fraser.
334 (top, both images) Australia / Eckersley Garden Architecture; (middle) Italy / Agape Design; France / Gérard Faivre; Australia / Keith McCutcheon, www.casaguardi.com; (bottom) Bali / AREA; USA / Carole Katleman Interiors; Brazil / Ruy Ohtake.
335 France / Jason Maclean. **336** France / Gérard Faivre.
337 (clockwise) USA / Kay Kollar Design / Chu + Gooding Architects; France / Gérard Faivre; Australia / Sharon Fraser. **338** Sri Lanka / Jack and Jo Eden, www.villasinsrilanka.com, www.joedenmimimango.com; Australia / Brian Zulaikha, Tonkin Zulaikha Greer.
339 Australia / James Russell; France / John Rocha.
340 Bali / AREA. **341** Singapore / Kerry Hill. **342** (top) USA / Kay Kollar Design / Callas Shortridge; Australia / Bloc Design; Australia / Frank Macchia; (bottom) USA / Aleks Istanbullu; Bali / AREA; USA / Kay Kollar Design / Callas Shortridge. **343** USA / Barton Myers.
344 Brazil / Barton Myers.; France / Gérard Faivre.
345 Brazil / Isay Weinfeld; USA / Marmol Radziner.
346 (clockwise) Bali / AREA; Australia / [illegible] USA / John Lautner / Marmol Radziner. **347** (clockwise) USA / Andres Ariza, MXA Development; USA / Todd Oldham; France / John Rocha; Brazil / Isay Weinfeld. **348** Sri Lanka / George Cooper, www.kahandakanda.com. **349** Bali / AREA.
350 Australia / Bark Design; USA / Ghislaine Viñas.
351 Australia / Milenko Mijuskovic Architect; Studio Arthur Casas. **352** Australia / Frank Macchia; USA / Todd Oldham; Brazil / Studio mk27; Brazil / Studio mk27.
353 Australia / Keith McCutcheon, www.casaguardi.com.
354 Brazil / Isay Weinfeld. **355** (clockwise) France / Gérard Faivre; USA / Xten Architecture / Randolph Duke, www.randolphduke.com; USA / Karim Rashid; Denmark / Rasmus Larsson; Brazil / Studio Arthur Casas.
356 Singapore / Ernesto Bedmar, Bedmar & Shi.
357 USA / John Lautner / Marmol Radziner. **358** (top) USA / Rios Clementi Hale; (bottom) Australia / Glenn Murcutt; Singapore / Kerry Hill; France / Gérard Faivre.
359 (clockwise) USA / Susan Minter Design; USA / Xten Architecture / Randolph Duke, www.randolphduke.com; Australia / Keith McCutcheon, www.casaguardi.com; France / Gérard Faivre. **360–61** Brazil / Studio mk27.
362 USA / Barton Myers. **363** Australia / Donovan Hill.

index

To my parents, Gilian and Maurice – thank you.

Over the years I have been given access to the most amazing homes all over the world, so a huge thanks goes to all of those homeowners, architects and designers for their part in *Living Modern*.

A special thanks to all the writers, stylists and producers with whom I have collaborated, including Dominic Bradbury, Georgie Bean, Graca Buena, Amanda Talbot, Jean Wright, David Robson, George Katodrytis, Liz Elliot, Hatta Byng, Owen Gale, Alison Gee, Tami Christiansen, Justine Osbourne and Anna Utzon, whose works appear through these images.

Thank you also to Phyllis Richardson, Lucas Dietrich, Jennie Condell, Sarah Praill and Jane Cutter at Thames & Hudson for their tremendous teamwork; and to the editors and staff of the magazines around the world for their continuing support of my work.

For my wife, Danielle, whose productions feature throughout this book, for her love and unwavering support.

Richard Powers

First published in 2010 in hardcover in the United States of America by Thames & Hudson Inc., 500 Fifth Avenue, New York, New York 10110

thamesandhudsonusa.com

Library of Congress Catalog Card Number 2010923288

ISBN 978-0-500-51525-9

Printed and bound in China by C&C Offset Printing Co. Ltd